Playbill Three

The *Playbill* series brings together new, specially
commissioned or adapted plays for use in schools.
The emphasis is on contemporary developments in
the theatre and allied media. The volumes are graded
in difficulty.

Also edited by Alan Durband

Edited by Alan Durband

PLAYBILL THREE

Hutchinson of London

HUTCHINSON & CO (Publishers) LTD
3 Fitzroy Square, London W1

London Melbourne Sydney Auckland
Wellington Johannesburg and agencies
throughout the world

First published December 1969
Second impression July 1970
Third impression May 1972
Fourth impression August 1974
Fifth impression March 1976

Sixth impression September 1978

Printed in Great Britain by litho by The Anchor Press Ltd
and bound by Wm Brendon & Son Ltd
both of Tiptree, Essex

ISBN 0 09 105420 6 (cased)
0 09 105421 4 (paper)

Contents

Acknowledgements

For permission to publish the plays in this volume the editor is grateful to the following authors and their agents: John Mortimer and Messrs A. D. Peters and Co for *A Choice of Kings;* Ray Jenkins and Miss Margaret Ramsay Ltd for *Boy Dudgeon;* Alan Plater and Miss Margaret Ramsay Ltd for *Excursion;* Alan Gosling and Harvey Unna Ltd for *A Dead Liberty;* Ronald Duncan and Eric Glass Ltd for *The Gift.*

No performance of these plays may be given unless a licence has been obtained. Applications should be addressed to the authors' agents.

Introduction

Playbill Three contains plays by John Mortimer, Ray Jenkins, Alan Plater, Alan Gosling and Ronald Duncan.

1 The Plays

John Mortimer's *A Choice of Kings* was originally written for television, but in its revised and shortened form it now clearly belongs to the theatre. The play is an historical reconstruction of events leading up to the Norman conquest, and is based on an event in the life of Harold which historians have never satisfactorily explained. In 1064, at the summit of his fortunes, he crossed the English Channel and was blown off course to Ponthieu, where the local Earl, Guy, captured him. Guy realised the value of his prisoner and took him to Duke William of Normandy. Duke William was Harold's closest rival for the succession to the English throne, and had been promised the crown by Edward the Confessor (who was childless and without hope of an heir) as early as 1051. Nobody knows for certain why Harold left England at this time, or what terms he made to secure his release. *A Choice of Kings* provides a plausible explanation.

Ray Jenkins' play *Boy Dudgeon*, an adaptation of a Third Programme radio play, has a contemporary setting. It developed from a real situation. A gang of hooligans had been terrorising the younger children at the author's comprehensive school. He persuaded the ringleaders to talk about themselves into a tape-recorder after school; he learned about their gang organisation and how they spent their time making nuisances of themselves around the neighbourhood. One boy in particular stood out. He seemed to be isolated from the others and when he could be persuaded to speak he was almost incoherent. Years afterwards, Ray Jenkins wondered what would happen to such a boy if he ever found himself in serious trouble. How could he defend himself with such a limited vocabulary? Would anyone have the skill and patience to communicate with him, fully and sympathetically?

Out of this germ of an idea came *Boy Dudgeon*. Dudgeon, a teenager found guilty of the callous murder of an old woman, is already in prison when Mr Cliffe, schoolmaster and psychologist, takes up his case. With the permission of the blind prison governor he sets out to loosen the boy's tongue, hoping to establish his innocence. Cliffe gains Dudgeon's confidence. The words flow. But the truth is expressed in 'words of acid'.

Jack and Ginny Flint in *A Dead Liberty* by Alan Gosling can't even tell the truth to save their lives. They are appallingly ignorant; so ignorant that as the author has said of them 'they do not realise what trouble they are in. They say funny things and do stupid things. This is because they were only taught to read and add. It is sad that they have worked so hard and been made to understand so little.' The Flints are pitiable victims of half-knowledge. What little they know about the laws of society has been picked up from popular newspapers, TV serials and pub chat. Ginny is utterly dependent on Jack, who incriminates them with all the confidence of an ignoramus as he spins his unnecessary lies. Funny though the Flints are, it is with horror that we listen to their final words of self-congratulation. Unaware of the trouble they have lied themselves into, they indulge in happy fantasies—tragic victims of their own stupidity.

Alan Plater's *Excursion* is, by comparison, a straightforward comedy. Originally written for radio, it spotlights three groups of football fans—Tom, Arthur and their wives; Terry and Pete, two teenagers; and Sheila and Bernard, a courting couple. The narrator, Norman, links the episodes and provides a running commentary. But *Excursion* is more than a play about a football match: it is a play about people and their relationships. The mystique of the match divides the men from the women, and the men from the lads. Perhaps Edie and Doris once tried, like Sheila, to share the men's enthusiasm for football. Perhaps Tom and Arthur once larked about as spectators like Terry and Pete. In a football crowd, there is the life and times of the world and his wife, told in weekly episodes 'from one to the next to the next . . . not black and not white; . . . mostly it's grey, just dull grey and ordinary . . .'

Percy Worsthorne, the eccentric hero of Ronald Duncan's verse play *The Gift,* is reacting against this very dullness in his futile campaign to bring culture to the masses. The football results, indeed, provide an ironic commentary to his martyr-dom; and Grandfather Tremlett, disappointed at failing to win the Treble Chance, reconciles himself with the thought 'that there will be another week, next week'. Percy is too good to live in a world of football pools and TV commercials. His values are outmoded: 'Love one another . . . Read Donne . . . Listen to Schubert . . .' He is an embarrassment and liability to his family, a thousand years before his time and, by Worsthorne logic, a Christ-figure who must die to preserve the values he so passionately believes in. He is refrigerated with his latest poem frozen on his lips. Geraldine completes it, and we note the religious symbolism. In the background, the TV set 'pursues its irrelevant and frivolous commentary'. . . .

2 The Playwrights

John Mortimer was born in 1923 and educated at Harrow and Oxford. After a period of writing and directing for the Crown Film Unit during the war, he took up law and was called to the Bar in 1948. In 1966 he became a QC. He has written six novels (one of which, *Three Winters,* became a radio play) but since his first play *The Dock Brief* won the Italia Prize in 1958 he has concentrated on drama. He has now written a dozen plays (amongst them *Two Stars for Comfort, I Spy, The Wrong Side of the Park, David and Broccoli* and *What Shall We Tell Caroline?*), several film scripts and a number of revue sketches.

Ray Jenkins was born in 1935. After graduating at Trinity College, Cambridge, he went to Paris on a French Government scholarship and then completed two years' National Service in the Royal Artillery. For over three years he taught in a London comprehensive school, moving on to a College of Education where he lectured for a further two years before becoming a full-time writer. He has written two stage plays, a dozen radio plays, twenty-one TV scripts (for *Z-Cars, The Troubleshooters, This Man Craig,* and others) and a number of scripts for educational radio and TV programmes. His book *The Lawbreakers* was written for Penguin. Ray Jenkins is married with two children.

Alan Plater was also born in 1935, in Jarrow-on-Tyne. He has lived in Hull since 1938, apart from four years at Newcastle University. He trained as an architect but gave this up some years ago to become a full-time playwright. He started in sound radio: *Excursion* is one of the many plays he has written for this medium. His television work includes scripts for *Z-Cars, Softly Softly, The First Lady,* and eleven other plays including a distinguished trilogy *To See How Far It Is* for BBC2. His *Close the Coalhouse Door* (written in association with Alex Glasgow) is a musical about the Durham miners, and indicates his interest in social documentary and northern culture; he has been associated with the anthology programme *Northern Drift* since its inception. Alan Plater lives in a large old Victorian house with his wife and three children and likes 'watching football and observing the social and economic scene'. He is also deeply involved in a scheme to launch a small theatre in Hull.

Alan Gosling was born in 1927, 'downwind of Bow Bells'. After his army service he took an apprenticeship in commercial art, beginning by sweeping floors and graduating in his early twenties as a freelance designer and consultant. Then he suffered an eye illness called choiditis. To overcome the obstacle of blurred vision he decided to become a writer. He worked in his bedroom for eight months before he sold a play. Alan Gosling now writes full time for TV and radio— many episodes of *Dr Finlay's Casebook* are his—and with his eye trouble now cleared up he lives 'like a poor squire in a Tudor farmhouse', with his wife, three children, and an army of geese, ducks and hens.

Ronald Duncan, the author of *The Gift,* was born in 1914. In 1953 he founded the Devon Festival of Arts, and in 1955 the English Stage Company, which took over the Royal Court Theatre, Sloane Square, and began a new phase in the history of English theatre. He is best known as a poet

and poetic dramatist. Amongst his many plays are *This Way to the Tomb, The Eagle Has Two Heads, Stratton, The Catalyst,* and *Abelard and Heloise.* He has published four books of poems, a dozen prose works, and his autobiography (1963). His principal recreation is breeding Arab horses.

A Choice of Kings

JOHN MORTIMER

CAST

WILLIAM, THE BASTARD
FITZOSBERN, THE STEWARD
ODO, THE BISHOP
THEOBALD, THE CHANCELLOR
ROGER OF MONTGOMERY
GUY OF PONTHIEU
HAROLD, THE EARL
YOUNG GODWINESON

All applications to perform this play, whether by amateurs or professionals, should be addressed to A. D. Peters and Co, 10 Buckingham Street, London WC2

A Choice of Kings

SCENE 1: *A castle at Rouen. The scene is the main hall of*
DUKE WILLIAM THE BASTARD's *castle. The hall is hard, dark
and stony. Norman arches and high doors stage L lead to the
twisting staircases and dark rooms of the castle. Stage R
another high doorway opens out to the sunlight; it is, during
the action of the play, mostly kept shut. There is one high
chair with a great sword against it, a tall crucifix over it:
Christ, bleeding, tortured, his hair plaited with thorns, is
carved on the Cross. In the middle of the room there is a table
set with food and drink for a single guest, clean clothes laid on
a chair. As the curtain rises the Normans are waiting, dark,
roughly dressed as a band of pirates, their hair short and shaved at
the back.* WILLIAM THE BASTARD, *their ruler, is in the high
chair, cleaning a nail and waiting.* ODO THE BISHOP, *his half
brother, is looking at the food. He is self-indulgent, lecherous
and enormously ambitious. Unlike* WILLIAM *he's finely
dressed and fearless. The other Normans present are* FITZOS-
BERN THE STEWARD, *tall, cold and correct;* ROGER OF MONT-
GOMERY, *a splendid soldier, loyal, unimaginative and devoted
to* WILLIAM, *and* THEOBALD THE CHANCELLOR, *a young
man in monk's habit, nervous, eaten up with ambition, unable
to tell if his newly invented post makes him a cabinet minister
or a secretary.*

*Two servants are standing by the door. At the table a
Norman girl, young and pretty, is standing with a jug and a
bowl of water, ready to wash the hands of the visitor they are
expecting.*

The year is 1064.

ODO [*lifting covers*]: Eel. Trout. Mutton. Duck. [*Sniffs*] Plump partridge . . . I wish I were a visitor.

ROGER: I'd give him poison.

ODO: What's that?

ROGER: I'd say cold poison.

ODO: Poison's no longer used in international relations.

ROGER: He invaded France!

FITZOSBERN: Four sailors and his young brother. It hardly sounds like an army.

ODO: And why should he land in Ponthieu? It's a horrible place. Thin-rumped women that smell of herrings.

ROGER: All right. Why did he come?

ODO: Isn't that what we're going to find out? Apricots! [*He picks one up from the table*] Mine won't ripen. It's been a damp year for apricots. [*Drops it, feels the clothes*] Soft . . . He has a fair skin naturally. Has he got a fair skin, William?

WILLIAM: As far as I remember.

[*There's a sound outside. A gate clangs*]

FITZOSBERN: What was that?

ODO: Probably our visitors arriving.

[*A shout and then knocking at the doors.* WILLIAM *nods.* FITZOSBERN *nods to the two servants. They go to the doors, slide back the bolts. The doors slowly open.* HAROLD, *naked and filthy, his hands tied behind his back, is pushed into the room. He is tall and blond, Earl of Wessex and the greatest man after the King in Europe's most civilised country.*

With him is his brother, also a prisoner of GUY OF PONTHIEU,
*a minor pirate who, with a few followers, enters to deliver his
prize to* WILLIAM]

HAROLD [*looks up at* WILLIAM *on the chair, smiles, his teeth
white in a dirty face and says, amused, relieved*]: William the
Bastard!

WILLIAM: Harold, the Earl! [*He goes to* HAROLD, *puts his arms
round him, embraces him, turns to the servants*] Look after him.

[*Servants cut* HAROLD'S *bonds and the girl puts a robe on
him, washes his hands and face. In the foreground* GUY *speaks
to* FITZOSBERN, *who takes out a bag of money. In the
background* HAROLD *is being dressed and washed tenderly by
the girl*]

GUY: I thought the Duke might care to buy him eventually.
So naturally I kept him alive for you . . .

FITZOSBERN: He's starved as a sparrow!

GUY: It's not often we get an English Earl to ransom. A few
Abbots on the way to Rome usually . . . No one'll give you
a sausage for them. But a catch like him . . . Well, it makes
up for a thin crop of turnips . . .

FITZOSBERN [*looks at the money bag*]: He's underweight. You
ought to take a reduction.

GUY: Give me my price.

FITZOSBERN: There's no flesh left on him. Will you take six
hundred pieces?

WILLIAM [*calls across the room*]: Pay his price! [*To* HAROLD]
You shall be my honoured visitor.

[FITZOSBERN *gives* GUY *the money.* GUY *is on his way out with his followers. He stops to grin at* HAROLD *and bows*]

GUY: It was a pleasure to know you, sir.

HAROLD: I'd have paid you with a kick up the backside. Pirate!

GUY: Only a small landowner, sir. The living's terrible. What a disaster with the turnips!

HAROLD: Get rid of him!

[WILLIAM *signals.* GUY *is hurried out*]

WILLIAM: The sea breeds pirates . . . We have to live with them. Please sit down and eat.

HAROLD: And my brother?

WILLIAM: What?

HAROLD: He sailed with me. My mother's youngest.

[WILLIAM *moves towards him to embrace him.* YOUNG GODWINESON *flinches slightly*]

It is part of your education, boy. To be kissed by Frenchmen.

WILLIAM [*coldly—doesn't kiss* YOUNG GODWINESON]: You shall be given food. And clean clothing. [YOUNG GODWINESON *is taken out by a servant*] Sit down.

[HAROLD *goes to the table and sits. Picks up a bit of duck in his fingers, and is about to eat, when* ODO *starts intoning a Latin grace*]

ODO: 'O Dominus qui benedicat quinque panes in deserto . . .'

[*There is a pause.* HAROLD *takes a bite, but is frozen again*]

'Benedicite nunc hanc cibum.'

[*Again* HAROLD *takes a quick bite: but* WILLIAM *starts to present his court.* HAROLD *gnaws the food at last while holding out his hand to be clasped by the Normans*]

WILLIAM: My step-brother, Odo—Bishop of Bayeux.

HAROLD: You're the legitimate one, aren't you?

ODO [*unruffled*]: I hope you appreciate . . . all our dainties. [*He looks at the girl who is pouring the wine for* HAROLD]

WILLIAM: William Fitzosbern. High Steward of Normandy . . .

[HAROLD *clasps his hand, eating with the other*]

WILLIAM: My Chancellor. Theobald . . .

HAROLD: What's he do?

WILLIAM: He helps me draw up treaties.

HAROLD: Useful work.

WILLIAM: Roger Montgomery . . .

ROGER: I never shake hands with the English.

[HAROLD *looks at him gratefully and uses both hands to eat*]

WILLIAM: Leave us, gentlemen.

[*The Normans go*]

I thought you'd rather eat in peace.

HAROLD: It's unexpected.

WILLIAM: What?

HAROLD: I heard yours was a country full of swords and crucifixes—where you slept in chain mail and the dinner was—first course, a kind of porridge—second course, another kind of porridge. Someone's been teaching you English cooking! [*Pause*] I have to thank you, Bastard.

WILLIAM: Why?

HAROLD: You saved my life: and I'm very fond of it.

WILLIAM: I only paid your ransom.

HAROLD: Was I expensive?

WILLIAM: I think [*small smile*] . . . You were a bargain. Why did you come here?

HAROLD: I came for the fishing.

WILLIAM [*looks at him*]: Did you have a good catch?

HAROLD: No.

WILLIAM: No?

HAROLD: As a matter of fact . . . No. Tell you what . . .

WILLIAM: Yes?

HAROLD: We trailed the nets off Dover—you get good fish there usually—flat soles, fat mackerels, long lobsters if you're lucky. But the nets caught nothing but water. And then . . . it was after noon, the sun was high and the sea so flat . . . like a plate. And we saw a shoal, big plump silver fish swimming, waving their tails slowly. So we followed them—and the sea changed colour. Blue. Purple. And black. And still we saw that great shoal of fish swimming, very slowly but always just in front of us. So we went after them and they were jumping in and out of the water, flashing their tails and dancing, although they were big, heavy fish, you understand; but energetic, like fat girls dancing. And just then the wind came up howling, and blew us towards the sharp rocks off that beach at Ponthieu. And the fish turned tail and scattered. I heard them laughing, as the Pirate caught me . . . If you wanted to see me—you should've sent an invitation. Witchcraft was uncalled for.

WILLIAM [*crosses himself, upset*]: What're you suggesting?

HAROLD: Only that you control the fish, Bastard. Spiritually of course.

WILLIAM: I don't joke—about religious matters.

HAROLD: I'm sorry. But someone led me here—with a catch of mackerel. [*Sits, drinks. Looks at* WILLIAM *amused*] You're growing fat.

WILLIAM [*dignified*]: I eat very sparingly.

HAROLD [*taking more food*]: You should make love more often. Look at me. Three good meat meals a day and [*slaps his stomach*] hard as a board! And you're spreading like a pregnant mare . . . it must be a tight squeeze in the saddle.

WILLIAM [*taking this with a carefully controlled smile. He sits down by Harold*]: I've been expecting a visitor from England.

HAROLD [*looks at him closely*]: Why, Bastard?

WILLIAM: Because of something your Sainted King said to me. I remember he was showing me the plans of a Church he meant to build . . .

HAROLD: Oh my Sainted King; always building churches!

[*He rises, walks about the room drinking*] You know what this rain-water-eyed old man with his voice you have to strain your ears to hear in a high wind told me? [*Imitates*] 'I've had a vision, Harold.'

WILLIAM: Yes . . .

HAROLD: 'It's not a vision exactly, Harold—more of a visitation.'

WILLIAM: From whom?

HAROLD: It's always St Cuthbert! We're short of saints in England.

WILLIAM [*quiet, serious*]: Your King Edward told me—about his visitation.

HAROLD [*looks at him*]: He told you?

WILLIAM: 'The blessed Saint,' he said, 'has given me the name.' Those were his words to me.

HAROLD: What name?

WILLIAM: Who—should have England after him.

HAROLD: My country?

WILLIAM: Who should be King.

HAROLD: And who was it—Bastard?

WILLIAM: He wouldn't tell me then. He said—'When the time comes I shall send a messenger.' He said, 'When I see death clearly I will send a man to you in Normandy with the name.'

[*They pause.* WILLIAM *rises.* HAROLD *looks at him. Suddenly bursts out laughing*]

HAROLD [*rises. Goes to a window*]: When the wind's in the right direction can you smell England? [*To* WILLIAM] Does it make your mouth water?

WILLIAM: Why did you come here?

HAROLD: I came—with a message from the old man.

[*Long pause. The two men look at each other*]

WILLIAM: Whose name?

HAROLD [*quiet, almost a whisper*]: My name, Bastard. 'My throne,' Edward said, 'is for Harold, son of Godwin.'

WILLIAM: I thought you'd say that. So that's your message?

HAROLD: An offer.

WILLIAM: Make it.

HAROLD: To be under me as a Secondarius. The second power in the kingdom. My earldom and all its revenues. Sealed with a bond. Whilst I am King.

WILLIAM: Secondarius. And in return?

HAROLD: Let me peacefully take my throne.

WILLIAM: You're generous . . .

HAROLD: You accept?

WILLIAM: I'll consider it. You lied to me, however.

HAROLD: When?

WILLIAM: About the fish. If you lied how shall I trust you?

HAROLD: The fish . . . were a small matter. A fairy story. I'm not lying now. About King Edward's will. It's my name, Bastard.

WILLIAM: I tell you. A man came to my gate last year. A Holy man. In rags. He said, 'In December the world will end and you will be dead.' And he pulled out of his rags an old rusty key. One of St Peter's keys, he said, that would get me into Heaven. When the world ended in December. He wanted . . . I forget, one, two, gold pieces. For the Holy Key, you understand me.

HAROLD: It sounds something of a bargain.

WILLIAM: It would have been. If he'd told the truth about the end of the world.

HAROLD: What did you do?

WILLIAM: Kept him and his key in prison until after Christmas. We hanged him on the first of January. Your offer's generous, however.

HAROLD: You accept?

[WILLIAM *looks at him, then goes to the door and shouts an order.* FITZOSBERN, ODO *and* ROGER OF MONTGOMERY *come clattering in, followed by* YOUNG GODWIN, *washed and dressed in Norman clothing.* WILLIAM *picks up the great sword from by the chair*]

WILLIAM: Advise me. Tomorrow we fight Conan, a Breton rebel who doesn't appreciate the advantages our protection has brought his backward province. Conan's stationed in a valley with the hills behind him. In front there's a patch of marshland, useless for our cavalry. On the other three sides he's dug ditches with sharp stakes in them, so we can only charge him from the front . . .

HAROLD: What've you done so far?

ODO: Said a number of masses. The marsh hasn't dried up for some reason.

WILLIAM: Quiet brother! God's still with us . . .

ODO: Sometimes I wonder if He hasn't gone off on the Crusades. This is such a *small* battle.

HAROLD: Send your cavalry on to the marsh, a small force on light horses; but enough of them to look convincing. As soon as he attacks start the retreat: slowly so that he'll have to follow. That way you'll lead your enemy gently out from behind his ditches on to the soft ground . . . and when he's on the marsh cut him to pieces!

[*Silence. They all look at* HAROLD]

ROGER: We'll lose men at the beginning.

FITZOSBERN: Some'll get killed. Why else did they join the army?

WILLIAM [*faces* ODO]: What do you think, brother?

ODO: I think he's very devious, for a hero.

WILLIAM [*clasps his hand*]: You're a great general.

HAROLD: I've used it before. To bewilder the Welsh. It'll work well enough . . .

WILLIAM: It'll work. Tell our Captains.

[ROGER OF MONTGOMERY *and* FITZOSBERN *start.* WILLIAM *turns to talk to* ODO]

HAROLD: My plan, Bastard . . .

WILLIAM [*turning to him slowly*]: I accept it. Come here.

[HAROLD *walks slowly towards* WILLIAM. YOUNG GODWIN *watches intently*]

WILLIAM: You plan the wars and I'll make the treaties.

HAROLD: As my Secundarius?

[ODO *looks at them both*]

WILLIAM: There should be a Secundarius certainly. [*He raises his sword, for a moment it seems to strike at* HAROLD; *but he brings it gently down on to* HAROLD'*s shoulder*] But for my love, and today's services, I create you Harold of Wessex, son of Godwin: now Knight of Normandy.

[*Pause, then* HAROLD *bursts out laughing*]

HAROLD: Thank you, Bastard.

[WILLIAM *lowers his sword. Gestures to* ODO *and they go.* HAROLD *turns excitedly to* YOUNG GODWIN]

HAROLD: He believes me!

[*But* YOUNG GODWIN *looks at him unsmiling*]

GODWIN: He owns you now, Knight of Normandy!

HAROLD [*taking no notice of him*]: He believes my name's chosen. Edward won't know what message I gave him. Edward'll die and I'll be King of England!

GODWIN: You lied to him, and now he owns you. I'm going.

HAROLD: What's the matter?

GODWIN: To get a boat. I'll swim if I have to.

HAROLD: What do you mean?

GODWIN: He bought you—for a good meal and a Norman title.

HAROLD: Bought me? I bought him. I named the price and he's mine now. We'll sail home, and I'll walk to the throne without a hand raised against me!

GODWIN: I'm going . . . [*He goes to the outer door. Pulls at it*] It's locked. [*Pulls again*] They've locked us in . . .

HAROLD: Call the servants.

[YOUNG GODWINESON *runs to the other door. Pulls at it. It's locked also*]

Secondarius . . . my right hand!

GODWIN: We're prisoners!

HAROLD: Nonsense! [*He goes to the door. Hammers at it, calls*] Come here! Here. Boy! Here! Bastard! Come here, Bastard! Come when I call you! It's me now. Harold. Bastard! Come running. Listen! Can't you hear me? Let us out! [*Silence. No sound. They're locked in. Prisoners*]

GODWIN [*looking at* HAROLD]: Who'll pay your ransom now?

CURTAIN

SCENE 2: *When the curtain rises again the Normans are grouped round the table which has now the appearance of an altar, covered with an embroidered cloth.* WILLIAM *is seated in the chair,* ODO, FITZOSBERN, ROGER *and* THEOBALD *around him.*

WILLIAM: Three months, and he still spurns his oath!

FITZOSBERN: Three months, and we've been feeding him for nothing!

ROGER: What's the use of getting an oath out of an Englishman? He'll only break it.

ODO: Of course he will.

ROGER: What's the point of it then?

ODO: His breaking it, that'll be the point.

WILLIAM [*shouts a command to the servants*]: Bring him in!

[HAROLD *brought in from the doorway left; he's a prisoner, between two soldiers.* ODO *walks towards him*]

ODO: Have you anything to say to us?

HAROLD: Yes. The food's gone off. The first day I had duck and apricots. Since then all I've done is exhaust your varieties of porridge.

WILLIAM: Swear the oath, and you sail home tomorrow.

THEOBALD: Swear and covenant. You will in no way hinder the Duke of Normandy in his ascent to the throne of England.

[HAROLD *looks at* WILLIAM, *bursts out angrily at him*]

HAROLD: You tricked me, Norman! With your crucifixes and your brother in the Church and your soft offer of hospitality. Before God's face you lied to me.

WILLIAM: I never lied.

HAROLD: You lied like a horse dealer selling a lame mare to a blind man.

WILLIAM: Be careful.

HAROLD: Careful! Would you fight me? Would you get off

that chair and swing an axe at me? I'm ready. For three months I've been ready.

[*He moves forward as if he's going to strike* WILLIAM. *The guards hold him*]

WILLIAM: You can't strike. [*He gets up from his chair and moves to stand in front of* HAROLD]

HAROLD: No?

WILLIAM: Because of your lies.

HAROLD: My lies?

WILLIAM: What do you do in England in a case of murder?

HAROLD: Fix compensation for the victim's families.

WILLIAM: Don't you have a penalty? Death?

HAROLD: That hasn't occurred to us.

WILLIAM: You're in need of Norman civilisation. With us the murderer's hanged; after a fair trial, naturally.

HAROLD: What're you talking about, Bastard?

WILLIAM: The trial's a battle. If the prisoner's guilty his arms turn to water. The lies he's told weaken his sinews . . . the strength goes out of his knees and—he looks like a child. Really, it's comical. I've often seen it at trials I've attended. The foresworn have no heart in the fighting and the axe comes through their defence.

HAROLD: I don't follow the logic of Norman justice.

WILLIAM: Look. You've got no strength either.

HAROLD: No strength!

WILLIAM: The lies weaken the sinews.

HAROLD: I need some sunshine and English mutton. Let me go.

WILLIAM: You lied!

HAROLD: When?

WILLIAM: About the name!

HAROLD: Why should I?

WILLIAM: Because the name was William Bastard, Duke of Normandy. Edward sent you to give me his throne. That Holy Old Man . . .

HAROLD: Oh yes . . . that Holy Old Man.

WILLIAM: He never named the son of Godwin.

HAROLD: Let me go.

WILLIAM: Your talk of Secondarius. A trick.

HAROLD: I've learned better tricks here since I've been your visitor. Buy a man with a hundred gold pieces and then keep him like a squirrel in a cage.

WILLIAM: You came here to play a game with me. And it no longer amuses you. All right. It's over. Swear and go home. Sit in the sunshine, hug the long-necked peasant girl you daren't bring to church and wait for a king to come to England.

HAROLD: No.

WILLIAM: What?

HAROLD: What'll you have? My finger-nails? My thumbs

pressed to pulp? What do you need to force an oath out of me? A scream to flatter your sense of justice?

WILLIAM: Swear!

[*Pause.* HAROLD *spits in* WILLIAM'S *face. The Normans start forward, their hands on their swords.* WILLIAM *silences them with a gesture*].

WILLIAM: I shall have a little time alone with the Earl of Wessex. Let him be.

[*The Normans leave, grumbling. The guards go.* WILLIAM *goes to a side table and fills a cup with wine, brings it to* HAROLD]

WILLIAM: Drink.

HAROLD: I'm not thirsty.

WILLIAM: You think I've treated you harshly?

HAROLD: Not at all—you've been a perfect host.

WILLIAM: You laugh at me all the time.

HAROLD: You're wrong. I haven't laughed for three months.

WILLIAM: The last man to laugh at me was a soldier at the siege of Alençon. I saw him on the walls—he was holding out a bit of tanned leather and thumping on it like a drum. Thump. Thump. Thump he went. 'You know what this is?' he shouted. 'The way your mother carried on in the tannery the night Duke Robert stayed in Falaise.' My mother's family were connected with leather. [*He drinks. Then he puts the cup back on the side table*]

HAROLD: I understand the reference.

WILLIAM: I took that man myself. I formed up the Army and had his hands and feet cut off in front of the city walls.

HAROLD: You don't frighten me, Bastard.

WILLIAM: When they saw those bloody stumps, the city surrendered.

HAROLD: Is that why you're telling me this story?

WILLIAM: You've been lucky.

HAROLD: Eh?

WILLIAM: In your life, I mean.

HAROLD: Oh yes. It was a lucky wind blew me to France.

WILLIAM: Son of a great Earl. You grew up under the shadow of your father's sword.

HAROLD: What do you mean?

WILLIAM: You could ride out of his house free and safe, to go fishing or dance with the peasants or help with the corn harvest. Free to let people love you.

HAROLD: Love?

WILLIAM: I've seen them. When I was in England they'd come to the windows and cheer when you go past. The women throw flowers and the old men look at you with wet eyes. I never had time to be a hero.

HAROLD: You might have left a few more with their hands and feet. Perhaps they'd have cheered louder.

WILLIAM: I was fourteen; bastard son of a dead Duke with a poor, dark dukedom. Every lump of meat I ate might've choked me with poison. I saw my guardians die without explanation and I watched my tutor murdered the day we started Latin. The King of France hated me and every little Viscount wanted to sit in my chair. I have never had time for popularity . . .

HAROLD: Am I meant to weep now?

WILLIAM: But I had to learn, don't you understand? There's more to ruling than swinging an axe and riding back in a triumphant procession. So, I learnt government.

HAROLD: I never said you weren't successful.

WILLIAM: How to unite a country with promises, some to one, some to another. To make every man work for himself and everyone for you. To teach the King he was helping himself by helping me to beat the Viscounts, and teach the Viscounts how they could help themselves by helping me to be strong against the King. To know the power of every man and his one weakness: so they must all finally kneel down before my single purpose.

[*Pause.* HAROLD *looks at him with disgust*]

HAROLD: No-one would accept you! No-one in England. Whatever that old man said.

WILLIAM: So, it's true!

HAROLD: What?

WILLIAM: Edward named me.

HAROLD: What's it matter?

WILLIAM: He named me, yet he loves you.

HAROLD: What's love got to do with it?

WILLIAM: Oh yes he does. His eyes are hungry when he looks at you, and I've seen him when he wants to touch your hair, like an old man touching a child. He loves you, but he knows you'll never understand how to be a king.

HAROLD: Loves me? I've never thought about it.

WILLIAM: But together—don't you understand? I for the law to sit and judge and make a thousand quarrelling cut-throat princes know me Master. And for you, the hero, to ride at the head of the Army and through the smoking towns with flowers under your horses' hooves and cheers even from the ruins. Think of that . . . how we could rule . . . Not just England and Normandy but we'd go out, together . . . over France and Norway. Perhaps Hungary, even South . . . over the mountains. Into the South . . .

HAROLD: You mean kings together?

WILLIAM: You at my right hand always . . .

HAROLD: You mean . . . ?

WILLIAM: My Secondarius. Whom the people love.

HAROLD: So you could be hated in peace and quietness?

WILLIAM: A hero. For all Europe.

HAROLD: We might as well go off together arm in arm to the Holy Land . . . Look for your dead father under a few desecrated tombs.

WILLIAM: What I've proposed is perfectly practical.

HAROLD: And if we don't agree?

WILLIAM: You will agree.

HAROLD: But if I don't?

WILLIAM: There's no end to my hospitality.

HAROLD: So I'm your Secondarius or else your prisoner?

WILLIAM: Don't hate me. Simply because I've won there's no reason to hate me. Because I've won we can rule together. I'll always win when it comes to politics.

HAROLD: Me under you?

WILLIAM: Both of us. Under God.

HAROLD: I suppose you cut off that poor idiot's feet—in the name of Jesus.

WILLIAM: Certainly. Prayers were said on that occasion.

HAROLD: You make me vomit.

WILLIAM: You could pray now, also.

HAROLD: Before I lose my arms and legs?

WILLIAM: Before you turn your back on God's decision.

HAROLD: Has God decided I should be your prisoner?

WILLIAM: He sent you here. He lured you with a silver fish. When you said that, I should've believed you. I'm going now. I suggest you pray.

HAROLD: For a flash of lightning to burn you, Bastard.

WILLIAM: For a head half the size of your heart.

HAROLD: Bastard . . .

WILLIAM: Yes?

HAROLD: Those promises you made. Did you keep them all?

WILLIAM: As many as possible. As for the others . . .

B

HAROLD: Yes?

WILLIAM: I hope God will forgive me. Pray now, and reach your decision. [*Exit*]

[HAROLD *moves to the crucifix, stands in front of it, his arms wide apart*]

HAROLD: Lord of the sun. You've always been near me in the mornings, melting the icy shadows. After a night of aching wounds, cold and open, you've come to me with the soft new skin and the touch of velvet leaves. When I slept under a black oak tree at Waltham and the small, bitter snake gave me a kiss full of death you were there to suck the poison out through your glittering teeth and heal me with sunshine. You kept me clear of ghosts and witches and bad dreams and saved my wounds from rotting. When I was alone on the sea you sent me a wind and when I rode across the downs at night in search of my home you put out the stars to guide me. And in return I've never doubted you. I've put gold cups on your altars and planted fruit trees in your monasteries and washed the white, withered feet of your Holy Abbots. So now shine on me! Please. Melt these icicles. Let these dark doors fade away and the walls vanish. Let it be early morning and let me be standing in the garden of my home, talking to the Steward about the apple crop when the mist's gone and the sun's almost too hot for comfort. And over the wall I can hear my Edith Swan-neck and the children laughing and picking straw-berries for dinner, and all day it'll be summer with no work from London. Do you only care for the sick? Can't you manage a miracle for me?

[ODO *comes in quietly*]

ODO: You praying. The situation must be desperate.

[HAROLD *turns to* ODO—*looks at him disappointed*]

HAROLD: No miracle.

ODO: Alas—we can't expect them in political life.

HAROLD: Politics! I've been hearing about them from the Bastard.

ODO: You couldn't have a better teacher.

HAROLD: I don't need his lessons.

ODO: He is, of course, a man of quite terrifyingly high principles.

HAROLD: Oh yes!

ODO: It flows, I think, from the unfortunate circumstances of his birth.

HAROLD: What're you talking about?

ODO: William feels he must make up for the somewhat generous conduct of our mother on a certain windy night in Falaise, by a strict code of moral behaviour.

HAROLD: A moral pirate!

ODO: He's even extremely strict on the clergy found with a stray peasant girl among their domestic animals. I've often felt the cold wind of his disapproval . . .

HAROLD: Will I rot here . . . till I'm an old man, like Edward?

ODO: Now you and I, if I might suggest it, are not over-burdened with moral considerations.

HAROLD: What?

ODO: What do you want most at the moment? To see England again; your horses; your garden; your dear little white-haired children; your common-law wife—I hear she's quite lovely. And then you want to get back to work at Westminster to further your very laudable ambitions. You want to hear the cheers of the English and sit down before your own roast mutton. Now against all that—what price the promises?

HAROLD: When he was fighting for his throne, the Bastard made promises. That's what he told me.

ODO: Many, many promises. Some, alas, didn't live through the winter.

HAROLD: Promises!

ODO: A political necessity. When they're made. But situations change.

HAROLD: Do you believe it?

ODO: What?

HAROLD: That God weakens the arms of the man who swears and lies?

ODO: I'm not sure. I've noticed that really strong murderers seldom get convicted.

HAROLD: A point of theology . . .

ODO: Yes?

HAROLD: If I promise to give you the King of Norway's gold ring. From his finger . . .

ODO: Yes?

HAROLD: And if it's not mine to give . . .

ODO: I understand.

HAROLD: Is that promise binding?

ODO: Ah, now you've touched upon a most interesting point of ecclesiastical law.

HAROLD: Have I?

ODO: Clearly you have a mind of some subtlety. I would say no-one could force you to keep a promise you can't perform, therefore . . .

HAROLD: Yes?

ODO: Such a promise would not be binding. In the eyes of God. What's the drift of your questions?

HAROLD: Now, if I promise the throne to William . . . I must swear . . .

ODO: With your hand on that table.

HAROLD: Why there?

ODO: Because, it's where we gave you hospitality.

HAROLD: This looks like an altar.

ODO: No, I assure you. Simply a table.

HAROLD: A table?

ODO: From which you ate duck. The first night you came.

HAROLD: Is this cloth sanctified?

ODO: A piece of local tapestry, purely secular.

HAROLD: He's sent you to talk to me.

ODO: I know what's on his mind.

HAROLD: You must be able to see in the darkness. He sent you! Tell me the truth, without theology . . .

ODO: William knows he can't keep you here.

HAROLD: He can't . . .

ODO: It doesn't look well. In the eyes of Rome. It makes my brother look . . . like a common pirate, holding you to ransom. Already there have been signs of disapproval from the Cardinal Archbishop. William likes to appear in the right always. That's how he wins his battles. This situation is very painful to him.

HAROLD: You're making me weep.

ODO: And yet he can't let you go for nothing. Some of the Council have voted for your death. He's got to pay some attention to our fire-eaters; to extract a simple promise from you and let you go—that would satisfy everyone.

HAROLD: A promise?

ODO: Almost a formality.

HAROLD [*hopeful, seeing the way out*]: In which God is hardly involved . . . ?

ODO: I've explained. It'll be quite a secular affair. Purely a question for your conscience.

HAROLD: Yes . . .

ODO: Which has, I am quite sure, it's own priorities. There's been a fresh wind from the east since Saturday. You should make good time to England.

HAROLD: All right—call the Bastard back again.

CURTAIN

SCENE 3 : *All the Normans are on stage,* HAROLD *and* WILLIAM *are facing each other across the table, still covered by the cloth.* THEOBALD *is reading from a paper.*

THEOBALD : I, Harold Godwineson, Earl of Wessex, hereby solemnly swear and covenant that I will in no way hinder the Duke of Normandy in his ascent to the throne of England. In return, I, William Bastard, Duke of Normandy, will create the Earl my Secondarius under me in the Kingdom, giving to him all the Earldoms of Wessex, and Mercia together with Wales. Together with the hand of my daughter Agatha in marriage . . .

WILLIAM : I swear.

HAROLD : I swear.

ODO [*moving between them, places his hand on the cloth*]: Given at Rouen in the year of Christ, one thousand and sixty-four. This binding oath was sworn with due solemnity over the most sacred and Holy relics of Christendom, being the bones of our martyred saints now elevated to the Right Hand of God to bless the righteous man and punish the liar and perjurer, to weaken his arm and consign his soul to the Justice of everlasting damnation.

HAROLD [*afraid*]: What?

WILLIAM : We are sworn.

HAROLD : What're we sworn on, Bastard?

WILLIAM : Show him!

[ODO *and* THEOBALD *pull the cloth away. It has covered a shallow box on the table, filled with bones and the relics of saints.* HAROLD *is trembling, speechless, terrified by the solemn relics*]

THEOBALD: By the thigh bone of the Blessed St Catherine martyred on the wheel for Christ. By the finger of St Joseph of Arimathea. By the Holy Ribs of the Blessed St James. By the hair of the sanctified St Elfreda and the chain that bound the Apostle Peter. By the hard nails and the wood of the True Cross you are sworn. By the love of God and the power of the Holy Spirit and the Sacrifice of Jesus Christ, you are sworn.

ALL NORMANS: They are sworn.

ODO: Amen.

WILLIAM: Amen.

[HAROLD's *fear is primitive and total. He can hardly speak*]

HAROLD: Amen. Cover them up.

[FITZOSBERN *comes up to him, as if he were talking to a sick man or a child, puts a hand on his shoulder*]

FITZOSBERN: The ship is fitted and ready. You shall have the use of our best sailors . . .

HAROLD: Cover them . . .

FITZOSBERN: Although, naturally, we rely on your word, given with such solemnity, we shall, according to our usual practice in important treaties, require a hostage.

HAROLD [*to* WILLIAM, *pleading*]: Bastard . . .

FITZOSBERN: In these circumstances, we have decided that your young brother shall stay here on your return to England. He will be well treated; but he will be a guarantee that the terms of this agreement are observed, both as to the letter and the spirit. Harold, Earl of Wessex, is that agreed? Do you agree?

HAROLD: What?

FITZOSBERN: Your brother.

HAROLD [*all fight gone out of him*]: I agree. The bones . . .
Please, Bastard. Please. Have them covered up again.

[WILLIAM *makes a gesture. Attendants cover the bones*]

WILLIAM: The strength's gone out of him. The trial's
over.

[*He goes to the door L and goes out, two other Normans
follow him. Alone HAROLD goes to the chair and sits, weak
and helpless. He looks up as YOUNG GODWIN comes in from
the castle; he's smiling delightedly as he comes up to HAROLD*]

GODWIN: I never thought I'd sleep late this morning.

HAROLD [*looks up at him slowly*]: Why . . . ?

GODWIN: We're going, aren't we? They told me. The ship's
ready, they said. They'll think we're ghosts, won't they, at
home? I mean, they must believe we're drowned. Or that
the Pirate killed us. So when we walk in at the door they'll
know we're ghosts. That's what I'll say to Gyrth. I've
come to haunt you, brother . . . for stealing my Norwegian
pony . . .

HAROLD: I had no choice.

GODWIN: Oh, I know. I mean, you don't have to keep the
oath, do you?

HAROLD: I must go back. Edward won't live through another
winter, and when he dies I must be there in Westminster,
standing by the throne. My throne. You agree about that,
don't you . . . ?

GODWIN: Of course. Will they give us our swords back, do you think?

HAROLD: And when I'm King, I'll cross the Channel and fight the Bastard—it won't be long. I swear. It won't be many months even. What's a year at your age?

GODWIN: What're you trying to say?

HAROLD: I was right, wasn't I? There wasn't anything else I could do.

[*There's a sound of trumpets. The doors right are pushed open, sunshine streams in.* ODO, WILLIAM *and* ROGER *are standing there. They move towards* HAROLD. *As they do so* FITZOSBERN *also comes in behind them*]

FITZOSBERN: The boat's ready.

WILLIAM: There's a good wind, and the sun's shining.

ODO: This is a mournful occasion. You seem to have become quite one of the family.

HAROLD [*rises*]: You lying priest! You said the cloth wasn't sanctified.

ODO: It wasn't. The relics were beneath it.

HAROLD: You lied.

ODO: To tell some of the truth is not to lie.

GODWIN: Shall we go now?

[WILLIAM *moves towards* YOUNG GODWINESON. *Takes his arm*]

WILLIAM: I shall treat him as if he were my son entirely.

GODWIN: What do you mean?

WILLIAM: You shall have good hunting here, boy, and we'll teach battle and how to make peace. You'll learn Latin, I promise you, and in the autumn you shall travel with me to Rome.

ODO: I myself will be responsible for his spiritual welfare.

WILLIAM: I shall treat him, in all respects as if he were my son . . .

GODWIN [*to* HAROLD]: You didn't tell me.

HAROLD [*helpless and guilty*]: I didn't know. They sprung it on me like a trap. After I'd given all the other promises. Only one of us could go. Only one of us. I had no choice.

GODWIN: Did you think I wouldn't understand?

HAROLD: They didn't give me any alternative.

GODWIN: Of course it must be you. You'll be the King, Harold. Whatever they do to me, you'll be the King. I don't mind what they do to me. But couldn't you have told me, Harold? Couldn't you have said?

WILLIAM: Take him now.

FITZOSBERN: Come with me, boy, I'll take you hunting.

GODWIN: I'll be all right, till you come back for me. Be strong, Harold. Don't blame yourself.

FITZOSBERN: Come with me, boy.

[*He leads* YOUNG GODWIN *out left*]

ODO: The door's open, Earl of Wessex. Your ship's waiting.

WILLIAM: When Edward dies, you shall hear from me. Until then, Harold, the Earl . . .

HAROLD [*with a great effort, regaining strength*]: Until then, William the Bastard. And you shall hear from me . . . [*He turns towards the open door right and goes out slowly*]

ODO: It will work just as I said. He'll never feel easy now, using the name of king.

ROGER: And I said you should never've let him go. When Edward dies he'll call himself King of England just as if he'd never sworn at all. And you'll have to fight for your throne all over again: with axes! You can't trust the English. It always has to be a battle. . . .

ODO: A battle: of course. But don't you understand? It'll be a battle in which he feels the hand of God against him. Not a war any longer; but a trial in which he knows he's guilty. His arms'll turn to water.

WILLIAM: What did you say?

ODO: I said, he'll break the oath, but the oath will break him also.

WILLIAM: I suppose so. But if only he could keep it. If he could keep it, brother, what a pair of kings we'd make! The Earl and the Bastard. Together.

THE END

Boy Dudgeon

RAY JENKINS

CAST

GOVERNOR HALLIS
SEELEY
MR CLIFFE
ANTHONY DUDGEON

Boy Dudgeon

SCENE: *The juvenile wing of a prison. The stage has two acting areas. Stage Left: The Governor's Office. It has a leather-topped table with a large glass ashtray, chairs, a filing cabinet, and a presentation case of pinned butterflies. There are two doors; one leads to the centre of stage and the other off. Stage Right:* DUDGEON'S *cell. It has a bed, bedside locker and slops bucket. Between the cell and the audience is a wooden black frame of cell bars.*

DUDGEON and PRISON OFFICER SEELEY *march in and come to a halt outside the* GOVERNOR'S *office.*

SEELEY: Off with them boots smartish—no fiddling!

[DUDGEON *takes off his boots, his hands bothered by the manacles*]

And when you're inside, speak up clear. [*He straightens himself and knocks on the door*]

GOVERNOR: Come in.

[SEELEY *enters*]

SEELEY: 3434 Governor's Report, sir!

GOVERNOR: Right.

[SEELEY *about turns, collects* DUDGEON, *and marches him into the office*]

Are his boots off, Mr Seeley?

SEELEY: Yes sir.

GOVERNOR: Unlock him.

SEELEY: Sir. [DUDGEON'S *manacles are undone*]

GOVERNOR: Leave us completely alone. I want this boy to myself.

SEELEY: Sir?

GOVERNOR [*gently*]: The second time of asking, Mr Seeley.

SEELEY: Sir! [*Exits*]

GOVERNOR: Stand straight, boy.

[*Pause*]

[*Patiently*] Heels together. Good. There's a chair to your right, boy. Sit down. Good. Now extend . . . stretch out your legs. Excellent. Let the toes touch my instep. Good. [*Pause*] Now I'm the Governor, my name's Hallis, and as you see, I'm blind. A blind old man. My hobby is butterflies —hence the cases here. Now you—you're a stupid young thug. So we know all there is to know about each other. You can't even reach for that ashtray without—Sit still! [*Pause*] Dudgeon . . . in my first fortnight here I've seen every prisoner but you. No-one's different in a prison but I've kept you till last. Any idea why?

BOY: No, sir.

GOVERNOR: Good. Now. Feel your hands, boy . . . your palms. What are they—rough, smooth, calloused, splintered . . . a musician's?

BOY: Roughlike, sir.

GOVERNOR: Of course—you were a brickie. But that's all over for a time, isn't it?

BOY: Sir.

GOVERNOR: Are your hands strong?

BOY: Middling, sir.

GOVERNOR: Strong enough to grip steel, iron netting, pavement slabs, or lug lime bags. I used to watch boys like you build houses . . .

BOY: I was a brickie's mate, sir.

GOVERNOR: You were.

BOY: I were, sir, yes. [*He moves his foot*]

GOVERNOR: Don't move your foot, boy. Good. You're moving from here Monday morning—eight o'clock.

BOY: Where's that, sir?

GOVERNOR: You'll be told. As you know, this place isn't permanent, it's an Allocation Centre. Had your offence been less you might've made an Open Prison. As it is, it's bars. You afraid, son?

BOY: No sir.

GOVERNOR: Of course not. A lad who clubs an old lady to death's not likely to be worried by a train journey, is he?

BOY: Sir, I— [*Pause*]

GOVERNOR: Permission to speak.

BOY: I don't like trains.

GOVERNOR: Sir.

BOY: Sir.

GOVERNOR: Why?

BOY: Dunno.

GOVERNOR: That's not a reason.

BOY [*fumbling*]: My old woman threw herself out of one coming back from the 'op picking.

GOVERNOR: Oh yes. Nine years ago.

BOY: Sir.

GOVERNOR: But you'll still be going by train, I'm afraid. [*Pause*] I must say your silence during the trial was in some ways quite impressive, Dudgeon. But from your records here you seem to me plain thick. Why didn't you open your mouth? [*Pause*] I asked you a question.

BOY: They said I was guilty.

GOVERNOR: Who? Who?

BOY: Everybody.

GOVERNOR: That's over fifty million people, boy.

BOY: The blondies.

GOVERNOR: The police?

BOY: Sir.

GOVERNOR: When did they say this?

BOY: All the time . . . before and after, sir.

GOVERNOR: When? Behind your back, in the cell, in the toilet?

BOY: All the time . . . it was in their lamps all the time!

GOVERNOR: Don't shout—you'll worry Mr Seeley. So they said it with their eyes. Do I?

[*The* GOVERNOR *removes his glasses.* DUDGEON *gives a horrified gasp*]

Vitriol. They used to say I had calm, understanding eyes, boy . . . but they're not pretty now, I know. [*The* GOVERNOR *replaces his glasses*] But there's one blessing—put your foot back—they can't accuse, and they don't. Perhaps they even think you're innocent in your way. Are you?

BOY: What, sir?

GOVERNOR: Are you innocent?

BOY: Yes sir.

GOVERNOR: Despite evidence? Despite the trial?

BOY: Sir.

GOVERNOR: Good. You will remain isolated until Monday morning. I might be sending someone to see you. [*He calls*] Mr Seeley! Stand up, boy.

[*Enter* SEELEY]

Get this grey thing out.

[SEELEY *and* DUDGEON *exit. The* GOVERNOR *rises and opens the other door.* CLIFFE *enters. Outside,* DUDGEON *puts his boots back on*]

CLIFFE [*stubborn*]: I still think something can be done.

GOVERNOR: Not now, Bob, not now it can't. There's always a time for doing something, a time when something can be done. But the time the Dudgeons of this world reach here, that moment's passed.

CLIFFE: It was a gang affair.

GOVERNOR: Then why aren't they in with him?

CLIFFE: Because he kept his mouth shut.

GOVERNOR: For which he pays—

CLIFFE: The evidence seems to me inconclusive.

GOVERNOR: Ninety-nine per cent of the time it is.

CLIFFE: That's why the judging of a man needs to be the result of more thought, less speed, more examination—

GOVERNOR: We must not judge?

CLIFFE: No. To judge is to kill.

[*Pause*]

GOVERNOR: Bob, you good men—and I mean that—are wrong for one simple reason. You believe you are absolutely right. Yet you ignore facts, economics and human nature. Kindness and interest in the killer is self-indulgence without one scrap of social value. Dudgeon and his relatives distrust the helping hand. It leaves them uneasy and suspicious—because it sweats . . .

CLIFFE: Thank God you're lying!

[GOVERNOR *laughs richly and humanely*]

I know it's irregular, but I'd still like to talk to him.

GOVERNOR: Well, it's up to you. You've got till Monday, then he's away.

CLIFFE: Thanks. I—

GOVERNOR: Bob, I've been in this business long enough to tell you one thing—why I can go through the day with an easy conscience. Every man I've governed—if that's the correct word—every man jack of them, sooner or later condemned himself out of his own mouth. The words in acid . . .

CLIFFE: Never a mistake?

GOVERNOR: Yes. [*Dropping his glasses slightly*] He did this to me.

CLIFFE: Sorry.

GOVERNOR: Why? It was my mistake and I've learned my lesson. Justice works to its own rules. We only follow and it justifies us. You think the boy's innocent. Good. Maybe I do. But it doesn't bother me one way or the other. It shouldn't. I've got a job to do.

CLIFFE: Thank you, sir.

GOVERNOR: You can use this room. [*Calling*] Bring him back in, Mr Seeley.

[DUDGEON *is led in by* SEELEY. *The* GOVERNOR *and* SEELEY *leave by the other door. Silence*]

CLIFFE: I want to help. [*Pause*] You must realise my position's a bit difficult. I'm not a doctor or a psychologist. I'm just . . . well . . . a friend of the Governor's.

BOY: One up for you, mate.

CLIFFE: He's let me come and talk to you. I want to help. Well? Nothing between us goes further than these four walls. Agreed?

[DUDGEON *stares, hostile*]

I already know quite a lot about you and the others who were up—Rollball King, Buchanan, Nelson—

BOY: Him!

CLIFFE: Yes. I interviewed him, too. He was quite helpful. He told me—

BOY: I bet he did an' all! Well, he got off! Me an' 'im's like that. [*He makes a short karate chop*]

CLIFFE: Why?

BOY: 'Cos—

CLIFFE: Have a cigarette. [*He slides a pack along the table*]

BOY: Why?

CLIFFE: You smoke.

BOY: So what?

CLIFFE: Then have a cigarette. Go on.

   [DUDGEON *takes one*]

BOY: What're these then, eh? They're all flat!

CLIFFE: They're Turkish.

BOY: Lovely!

CLIFFE: Light it yourself.

BOY: I—

CLIFFE: Matches are there.

   [*He puts down a box.* DUDGEON *lights the cigarette, watching* CLIFFE *closely, afraid of tricks*]

BOY: Ta. It's weird.

CLIFFE: What—lighting one for yourself?

BOY: Yeh. In the yard I 'ave to go to that to berk Seeley. He makes it like begging—just for a drag.

CLIFFE: While you're here you're regarded as dangerous.

BOY: So!

CLIFFE: So they do the striking.

[*Pause*]

BOY: Take more than a match to burn this lot down.

CLIFFE: What would?

BOY: Bucketful 'a atom bombs.

CLIFFE: Would you if you could?

BOY: You kiddin'!

CLIFFE: Why?

BOY: It stinks. All them pans an' soap.

CLIFFE: You miss home?

BOY: You would 'n all!

CLIFFE: I live on my own.

[*Pause*]

BOY: What are you, then?

CLIFFE: I'm a schoolmaster.

BOY: Why ain't you at school then, eh? Lose your mark, you will, if you don't hurry. What you on me for?

CLIFFE: Two years ago a boy of mine was convicted unjustly because I couldn't be bothered to help.

[DUDGEON *is unimpressed*]

BOY: What did Halfy say?

CLIFFE: Nelson? Oh, he just told me about the gang. You know. [*He takes a pair of maraccas from his grip*]

BOY: No I don't. What're them?

CLIFFE: Maraccas.

BOY: M-what-ers?

CLIFFE: Maraccas—they're used for rhythm.

BOY: I know—I saw them in a Kit-E-Kat Band once.

CLIFFE: You don't like coloured people?

BOY: They're all right I suppose—'cept when they're in a bunch.

CLIFFE: Try them.

BOY: Why?

CLIFFE: Go on. There's no harm, no trick.

BOY: Do they test something about me then, eh?

CLIFFE: No. Look. [*He plays the maraccas well*]

BOY: That's good—you like trad?

CLIFFE: No, modern mostly.

BOY: Who?

CLIFFE: MJQ. Hamilton. A bit of Mulligan.

BOY: They ain't got no beat. It's all in the air, like that stuff on Christmas trees—tinsel—

CLIFFE: It's got beat all right . . . only it's not so obvious.

BOY: My old man thinks it's pretty.

CLIFFE: And you always believe what your father says?

BOY: He's been around. He's a good bloke.

CLIFFE: How's your father going to manage the fish shop without you around?

BOY: He'll get some berk.

CLIFFE: Can he afford another help?

BOY: Him? He's got more money 'n . . . He was going to buy me a place next year. Start a chain 'a Dudgeon fish bars.

CLIFFE: How much did he pay you?

BOY: Same's what I got on the buildings before I stopped— £14, Sunday and Monday off.

CLIFFE: Why did you stop?

BOY: Felt like it. Wanted to work for the old man.

CLIFFE: On these nights you'd meet Nelson and King?

BOY: Not always.

CLIFFE: Were you afraid of Nelson?

BOY: Him? Me? Nah! Why?

CLIFFE: He's older, bigger. You're quite small.

BOY: He bet me once—

[*Pause*]

CLIFFE: What did he bet you?

[DUDGEON *has picked up the maraccas*]

Yes, go on—play.

BOY: Can I?

CLIFFE: Sure—go on.

[DUDGEON *has an immaculate sense of rhythm. Delighted, he begins to experiment*]

Do you like music?

BOY: Hah! My old woman used to play the violin.

CLIFFE: Professionally?

BOY: Nah! M'dad stepped on it once and she never got it mended.

CLIFFE: You liked your mother.

BOY: Never saw much of her, did I?

[*Pause*]

CLIFFE: You didn't mind the smell of fish?

BOY: It washes off. Not like this place. It stinks.

CLIFFE: Why?

BOY: It stinks—that's all I know. Can I go now? [*He puts down the maraccas*]

CLIFFE: Yes. If you're innocent, let's prove it. Get you out, out of the smell . . . it's simple enough. See you.

BOY: All right.

[*The lights of the* GOVERNOR's *office fade as others come up on the cell: outside it stands the* GOVERNOR, *an overcoat behind his back.* SEELEY *hurries up*]

SEELEY: Sir! [*Breathless*] I was down A Wing, sir!

GOVERNOR: Ah, Mr Seeley. Open this a minute.

[SEELEY, *bewildered, opens the cell door. They enter*]

Sit down. Good. Now please relax. I've called you off duty for a second because I want to ask you a few questions.

SEELEY: Sir. [*He looks worried as the* GOVERNOR *locks the door*]

GOVERNOR: We often lock up, but we're rarely locked up. [*Silence*] You've seen a lot of service, officer.

SEELEY: Twenty-one years, sir, 'cluding wartime.

GOVERNOR: And never been promoted?

[SEELEY *freezes*]

Never mind. You've seen men come and go . . . with indifference?

SEELEY: I'm sorry, sir—I don't quite—

GOVERNOR: You've never become involved? Their condition has never given you cause to doubt the rightness of what you're doing?

SEELEY: I've had me orders, sir—plain and clear.

GOVERNOR: You've gone by the book, Mr Seeley!

[SEELEY *stands*]

SEELEY: Yes sir.

GOVERNOR: Sit down. [*Pause*] I'm interested in Dudgeon, Mr Seeley. The picture I get of him is built up from theory, you understand. You on the other hand supervise the emptying of his pans—the scrubbing of his bed. I'm not so close as you. Do you like him?

SEELEY: No sir.

GOVERNOR: Do you dislike him?

SEELEY: No sir.

GOVERNOR: Then why do you steal his dog-ends?

SEELEY: I don't sir!

GOVERNOR: LIAR! Officer, Mr Cliffe's brand are not on general issue. I know Dudgeon only smokes halves. The rest he dogs away. Mysteriously these reappear in your overcoat pockets—

[*The* GOVERNOR *throws the coat into* SEELEY'*s lap*]

SEELEY: He beat up the old lady!

[*Pause*]

GOVERNOR: Officer, Mr Cliffe is buying that boy's tongue with odd-shaped cigarettes. Keep your web-feet out. I want no inspection of Dudgeon's person until Monday. That's an order, Mr Seeley—plain and clear . . . out of the book!

SEELEY: Sir!

GOVERNOR: Sir!

[*The scene fades. Lights up on the* GOVERNOR'*s office*]

CLIFFE: You don't mind solitary—being on your own?

BOY: 'Salright.

CLIFFE: You don't miss people?

BOY: Why should I—they ain't 'ung flags for me.

CLIFFE: They've condemned you. They've judged you.

BOY: Then thas their lookout, en'it?

[*Pause*]

CLIFFE: What do you do with yourself?

BOY: I go to the races in me top hat.

CLIFFE: Then?

BOY: I reads till they puts the lights out.

CLIFFE: What?

BOY: *Pilgrim's Progress*—'s too hard tho'—all the words are old and mad.

CLIFFE: Do you think about yourself? The prison? Your father?

BOY: No—only fags.

CLIFFE [*laughing*]: Catch.

BOY: You're on the ball!

CLIFFE: Sometimes.

[DUDGEON *lights his own cigarette and offers one to* CLIFFE, *who shakes his head*]

What about the gang?

BOY: What about them?

CLIFFE: Look, boy, you're in a mess. I'm trying to help and it's not easy. I know a lot about you but I need to know a lot more—the truth for instance—and I have to drag everything, every dot and comma, from you.

BOY: Thas your job, mate! Thas why! I'm tired 'a questions, see! Everybody, the old man, the ancient upstairs, the blondie at the door—"Is he in?" . . . "Where was he that Saturday night?" . . . "What was he wearing?" . . . "Why ain't he on the buildings no more?"—

CLIFFE: Then you *were* out that Saturday night?

BOY: 'Course I was . . . I'm always out Saturday nights, but I wasn't where they said I was. I was somewhere else—

CLIFFE: Where? [*Pause*] Where? At the trial you said you were indoors.

BOY: An' you! You ain't stopped! Every nit in London's had a go—"This is Your Bloody Life"!

CLIFFE: Only I'm trying to help.

BOY: You're sorry for me, aint y' ?

CLIFFE: Yes, I am.

BOY: My tongue ain't good enough, is it? The rain's coming in through my roof, ain't it? That's what you think, ain't it?

CLIFFE [*patiently*]: "To be detained during Her Majesty's Pleasure". You've been condemned in a court of law.

BOY: I know. I was there, sitting with me two uncles in blue suits—

CLIFFE: Dudgeon—legal language's different language. Full

of tricks and alleys—to speak it you have to learn it and think in it and speak back in it. It's not like a foreign language—you can't get away all the time with just pointing. Do you understand? [*Pause*] Sometimes, though, you can get someone to point for you—interpret—but always, all along the line, you need help.

BOY: Thas why I shut up.

[*Pause.* DUDGEON *flicks ash on the floor.* CLIFFE *slides the ash-tray to* DUDGEON]

CLIFFE: Use this.

BOY: This is real heavy.

CLIFFE: It does a heavy job.

BOY: I could do you in with this.

CLIFFE: Yes.

BOY: My 'and's big, see. Big for me age. I can hold it in one hand. [DUDGEON *circles the room threateningly*] It fits neat like a bomb. [*Pause*] I could do you in with this. [*Pause*] Couldn't I ?

CLIFFE: Yes.

BOY: Yeh—nobody's here . . .

CLIFFE: Only Mr Seeley outside.

BOY: Just us, see.

CLIFFE: And your boots're off—

[DUDGEON *is now behind* CLIFFE]

BOY: I could walk up behind y'. You wouldn't know 'cos you're not looking.

[CLIFFE *doesn't turn. For a moment,* DUDGEON *is tempted to hit* CLIFFE *with it*]

But I'm not going to, 'cos I don't do things like that. I saw a bloke at a fair once 'n Tooting Bec—he give the bloke ten shillings just to shoot at a doll—not the target. Bent, he was. [*Laughs uncertainly*] Why don't you look, eh? Look at my hand! [*Pause*] It's big, big for my age—why don't you look!

CLIFFE: Ashtrays're for ash.

BOY: LOOK AT ME! [*He smashes the ashtray violently on the floor. The door opens quickly—*SEELEY *enters*]

CLIFFE: Get out, Seeley!

SEELEY: Sir—

CLIFFE: Get out!

[*Door slams.* SEELEY *stays outside, uncertain*]

BOY: I'll pick 'em up. No, leave me—I'll pick 'em up.

[*The pieces are shuffled together carefully. We see* DUDGEON *hide a sliver of glass surreptitiously*]

CLIFFE: Put them here—that'll do.

[*Pause*]

BOY [*little-boy voice*]: What did Halfy tell you then, eh?

CLIFFE: Oh, lots of little things. At school you didn't like being pushed around—but there's lots of small boys like that. Then in the second year you were in their fourth-year gang.

BOY: Thas 'istory.

CLIFFE: You threw a can at a half-blind master.

BOY: Thas old stuff.

CLIFFE: Why did you?

BOY: He was old.

CLIFFE: What did he do to you?

BOY: He was old—thick—the berk!

CLIFFE: Nelson and Buchanan were thrown out for spitting into little girls' hair. Clever stuff! They said it was your idea.

BOY: But I never done it.

CLIFFE: And yet they almost let you join the gang after school. [*Pause*] Why couldn't you belong?

BOY: We 'ad to do something to' belong.

CLIFFE: So you pushed in a newly laid wall.

BOY: It was all new!

CLIFFE: That's why? That's the reason why?

BOY: Then they could see what I done! But the blondies're thick. They should've had me in for that. I got off, see!

CLIFFE: So they wouldn't let you join officially?

BOY: 'Cos'a some stupid rules!

CLIFFE: What rules?

BOY: Why d'you want to know?

CLIFFE: Interest.

BOY: You're writing a book or something about me, ain't y'?

CLIFFE: No—I'm working off my own guilt.

[*Pause*]

BOY [*sullen*]: You 'ad to be 'ad up.

CLIFFE: In court?

BOY: Yeh.

CLIFFE: An' then you were in the gang?

BOY: Only if it got a bit in the papers'n'all.

CLIFFE: What about the others?

BOY: Buck nicked a scooter, Halfy got in a furniture shop next to the Astoria, Rollball put his boot in a juke . . .

CLIFFE: This is your first up. Why didn't you get caught before?

BOY: 'Cos I got more up top than Nelson. Thas why.

CLIFFE: And he's working, and you're here?

BOY [*stung*]: YEH, WELL—HE DID IT, SEE—HE DID IT!

[*Silence*]

CLIFFE: What did you say?

BOY: Nothing. I never said nothing. Give us a fag.

[CLIFFE *pockets the cigarette packet*]

CLIFFE: Nelson did what?

BOY: You don't understand. [*Desperately*] Look, the time when the wall went over a blondie asked me where I got all the muck on me coat. See, Halfy had a mate called Mick—and he let me borrow his working leather—and they found that, 'cos I'd thrown it under the wall—so Mick got the blame. I told the blondie it was 'im.

CLIFFE: But you wanted to belong?

BOY: I know. But Halfy's mate got it. He got it.

CLIFFE: How does this connect with you being here?

BOY: They still wouldn't let me join! Halfy said I could join if I owned up. I said no. So they duffed me up. All of 'em. Then Halfy said he'd get me . . . and I said he hadn't got it up top. So he let me join the gang on purpose to get me. I know he did that. [*Pause*] So the next time, he did it. We got started on the grab-game. But he did it, Mr Cliffe. He got the old lady in the door . . . and that wasn't my job, see. He got Miss Phillips in the—

CLIFFE: Her name was Andrews—Miss Lilian Andrews—

BOY: It don't matter. Halfy got the old lady in the door. I didn't see it, see! I was in the gang, yeah, but I wasn't a full member. He did it. He thumped her head.

CLIFFE: How?

BOY: With the handle.

CLIFFE: The fingerprints were yours.

BOY: We all got handles!

CLIFFE: Nelson too?

BOY: All of us!

CLIFFE: What happened to the others?

BOY: How do I know! Scarpered!

[*A far-off clock chimes; the prison buzzer sounds;* CLIFFE *crosses and opens the door.* SEELEY *straightens up*]

CLIFFE: Mr Seeley.

SEELEY [*entering*]: Sir?

CLIFFE: Time's up.

SEELEY: Get up you—put your boots outside. Wonder the smell don't get you, sir.

CLIFFE: I've suffered worse. See you tomorrow, Dudgeon— and on Sunday.

BOY: I'm going on Monday.

CLIFFE: I know. See you tomorrow.

[*They exit. Absently* CLIFFE *plays the maraccas as the lights fade*]

[*Lights up on the cell* DUDGEON *is reading with the slowness of the semi-backward reader*]

BOY: 'As—I walk/ed—th/threw—the—wil/der/ness—of th/ this—w/world—eye—li/lighted—on a cer/tin—place— w/were—was a—den.—an'—layd—me down—in th/that— p/place—to sleep; an' as—eye slept—eye—dr/dreamed a dream.—eye—dr/dreamed—and be/hold eye saw—a man —cl/clothed—w/with—rags st/stand/ing—in—a—c/cert/ain —place—w/with—his—face—f/from—his own—h/house, —a book—in his—hand—a g/great—bur/den—upon his back.—eye—l/lookt, an/saw—'im—o/pen the—b/book— and—read—th/there/in;—and as he r/read—he w/wept— and tr/tremb/bled; and not—b/b/being—ab/el—longer to —con/tain, he b/breake—out w/with—a l/l . . . l/lamen/ men/tab/bul—cry—say/ing—wot sh/shall—eye do . . .'

[*Silence. Then there is a loud clanging of buckets and doors are thrown open*]

SEELEY [*off*]: Slops out! Stand by your doors! Move y'crabby lot! Slops out! Stand by your doors! An' move! [SEELEY *enters*] You can leave yours. It's talking time again. [*He marches* DUDGEON *off. Fade*]

[*Lights up on Governor's Office. This time* SEELEY *is seated in the corner*]

BOY [*laughing*]: 'Course, I laugh sometimes.

CLIFFE: Good.

BOY: What y' want to know that for?

CLIFFE: Oh, I don't know.

[*Pause*]

BOY: Hey—you know anything about dreams 'n things?

CLIFFE: A little, not much.

BOY: I keeps on 'aving this same dream—

CLIFFE: Go on—

BOY [*whispering*]: Why's Seeley here?

CLIFFE [*whispering*]: You have the habit of throwing glass about.

BOY [*starts whispering, but gradually forgets and speaks naturally, picking at the table edge with his nail*]: I keeps having this same dream. I'm in this train an' it's going dahn-hill. Then it starts going a bit too fast like. I'm the conductor, see, 'n all the ladies in black're looking at me. I goes along to the

engine but the driver ain't there. So I pulls the cord—an'
then—an' this is the bit I don't get—then all the old ladies
JUMP OFF and they all falls and rolls the wrong way and I
shouts 'Jump with the train'—an' then we hits a wall.
Everything's quiet. Dead quiet. And . . . all the old ladies
they comes up to me and says . . . can they have their
money back, and their shopping bags? I says 'you 'ad 'em
when you got off' and they just looks and says 'you're a
bad driver'. I says 'I ain't the driver. I'm the conductor and
they says 'you pinched 'er bags'. I says it ain't my job to
pinch their stinking old bags, and 'sides, there ain't much in
'em anyway, and they says—'we'll tell your mum 'a you'
and I says 'I ain't got a mum'. So I looks over the wall
and there're all the bags with all the money. Then all the
old ladies starts crying and I 'as to 'elp 'em over the wall,
but they can't cos they're old and their bones 're brittle and
break easy . . . so I starts to push 'em through the wall and
they says—'harder! harder! harder!' and they got big grins
on their mushes . . . and I wakes up. [*Silence*] Mad, in'it?

CLIFFE: Why're you asking me?

BOY: Dunno. Thought you might know, thas all.

CLIFFE: In your trial—never a single question. Why now?

BOY: Dunno. What's it all about then? You're a doctor.

CLIFFE [*annoyed*]: I'm not a *medical* doctor!

BOY: Seeley says you're interested in cases. [*Earnestly*] What
do I do, Mr Cliffe, if I don't want that dream coming back?

CLIFFE: You afraid of it?

BOY: A bit.

CLIFFE: You talk about it.

BOY: But I told you—

CLIFFE: I know—but that's just a start. Tony—fears, or things you're afraid of, even if you can't put a name to them—are things of the dark. To understand them, to see what they look like, how big they are, you have to bring them out into the light. That's what we helpers try to do.

BOY: How?

CLIFFE: We try to pin these fears to a board so to speak—like butterflies—and then we both look at them, discuss them, and when we know all about them we throw them away.

BOY: Or hang them on a wall.

CLIFFE [*laughing*]: That's it.

BOY: Why does the governor always draw butterflies—when he can't see them?

CLIFFE: That's his way of seeing them, I suppose.

BOY: He can't half draw, can't he? [*He picks up the maraccas and plays them*] What about my dream then?

CLIFFE [*pacing to and fro*]: Dudgeon, you've been very honest with me—you've told me a lot —your mother, your father, the shop, the gang—everything except one thing—

BOY: What's that then, Mr Cliffe?

CLIFFE: You've only once mentioned Miss Phillips.

[*The maraccas stop.* DUDGEON *puts them down*]

BOY: What you want to know, then?

[*Pause*]

CLIFFE: How old is she?

BOY: Hundred and seventy last Christmas.

CLIFFE: Do you like her?

BOY: She's old. Nah, I don't.

CLIFFE: She's your Godmother.

BOY: She was a friend of my mum.

[*Pause*]

CLIFFE: She spoke very highly of you the day of the trial—
your best witness.

BOY: She wanted me on her side.

CLIFFE: How much does she pay for the room over yours?

BOY: Ask me old man.

CLIFFE: Not much, is it?

BOY: Me old man likes 'er, that's all.

CLIFFE: Why?

BOY: Dunno. He does, that's all. He don't know she's after
him. But she won't get him—not me old man, he's been
around.

CLIFFE: Did you like this arrangement?

BOY: I 'ad to lump it . . . and move out 'a my room.

[*Pause*]

CLIFFE: Come on, boy—you can trust me now.

BOY: Me old man says, trust people 's far as you can spit them.

CLIFFE: Tell me about her.

BOY: She's a creeper—goes to church.

CLIFFE: Did she try to make you go?

BOY: Yes.

CLIFFE: Did you?

BOY: What, and sit with that lot—little old ladies an' little Bibles and everybody coughing their guts up!

CLIFFE: But you did her shopping for her?

BOY: How do you know?

CLIFFE: Trial evidence.

BOY: You seen her?

CLIFFE: Yes.

BOY: Well you know what she looks like. Look Mr Cliffe—I hates her flippin' guts and she knows it. Once I 'ad a party in 'er place when the old man was on business down in Brighton. Rollball and that lot mucked up the place and when they got out I come back in the house and sees her cleanin' up the mess in her dressing gown and Nelson all gawping and she lapped it up. Then he went. Then she stands there not smiling—she only smiles for Dad. She got on to me, mocking like, said I was treating the house like a breakers' yard. My 'ouse—not hers! Said I didn't respect Mum—an' where was me dad? I could see she was jealous like . . . on and on she goes like a ruddy gramaphone . . . so I smashed a glass . . . she picks it all up . . . only she kept one bit to show Dad ... [*Pause*] She says she'd say nothing if I did her groceries every Saturday morning ... and the gang give me the bird for that ... 'Where's your Bible, Dudge?' 'n 'how much's your old-age pension, Dudge?' 'n all that. So I says to her—do your own groceries—but she got the hook in proper ... on and on ... [*Mimics*] 'Everybody shops on Saturday, Tony ... an old woman gets banged about in the crush, Tony ... old people're afraid a 'buses and people pushin' 'em around ... our bones're more brittle ... and they break easy' so to shut her up I says yes. She 'ad me after that ...

CLIFFE: How?

BOY: Couldn't have a drag without her looking.

CLIFFE: Are you sure she's as hard as this?

BOY: She never smiles. 'Life's a joy Tony.' 'Every day's a gift ...' on and on and on. An' all the time she wants my old man. She does her nut when the old man has 'is birds in. He throws bottles around just for fun ... smashes 'em on the wall ... but she don't say nothing.

[*Pause*]

CLIFFE: And you think she took it out on you?

BOY: Yeah. She saw the lime on me coat after I pushed the wall in ... and when the blondie come to the door she says I was with her and he clears off.

CLIFFE: She saved you.

BOY: Yeah, but I couldn't get with the boys! I didn't have no chance. I couldn't get into the gang see ... and smash something up ...

[*Deadly quiet. Gradually* DUDGEON *will realise he is
confessing, but, hopelessly, he pushes on*]

Then they let me back in, all of a sudden, they let me be a
member. See, they was startin' on the grab game . . . an'
they wanted one more . . . I had me last chance . . .

CLIFFE: Whose idea was it?

BOY: Halfy's.

CLIFFE: Who chose the victims?

BOY: Rollball 'n Buck.

CLIFFE: Why them?

BOY: They done it before—they got experience.

CLIFFE: What did *you* do?

[*Pause*]

BOY: I asked old ladies the time.

CLIFFE: Where did you do all this?

BOY: Down the Wall.

CLIFFE: Always?

BOY: No. Wan' us to get caught? But it was the Wall most
times.

CLIFFE: How many times?

BOY: Two times.

CLIFFE: Who snatched the bags?

BOY: Find out.

CLIFFE: Which fool did the hitting?

BOY: If she yelled you mean? All of us. It was a gang see, an' we was all members, fully qualified. Buck whistled when one was coming, Rollball tracked, I asked the time 'n Halfy accidently knocked her into the wall. Then . . . the bag got grabbed and . . . I had to hit her soft, Mr Cliffe. That was my bit, the bit Halfy give me. But when this one started screaming straight off, Halfy clumped her too early . . . then he said nobody was in the gang if they didn't hit . . . 'n if anybody said anything he'd kill 'em and his brother was hung . . . for doing that, to another bloke, his mate.

[*Pause*]

CLIFFE: Where did the handles come from?

BOY: Rollball's in the building.

CLIFFE: Go on.

BOY: She screamed like hell, Mr Cliffe; she said God'd get me, just like Miss Phillips . . . then I HAD to hit her . . . it was her face all smiling like the dream . . . smiling . . . and I hit and hit till I was tired. That's what my dream's about ain't it . . . ?

[*Silence*]

CLIFFE: Nobody else hit—you know that, don't you son?

BOY: They scarpered. Left me looking at her.

CLIFFE: Are you sure they had handles? [*Pause*] Nelson told you not to bring them, didn't he? [*Pause*] Yours was the only one.

BOY: It was Halfy's really. He left it at the party.

[*Silence*]

CLIFFE: Tony—at your trial you said you weren't there.

BOY: Well I was, wasn't I? I said I was. I said I did it. You got Seeley here for 'Er Majesty's witness.

SEELEY: Time's up, sir.

CLIFFE: I haven't used Mr Seeley as a witness—

BOY: WHAT YOU ON ME FOR THEN?

CLIFFE: I thought you were innocent.

BOY: Well—I'm not.

CLIFFE: No!

SEELEY [*quietly*]: Put your boots on you, an' quick.

CLIFFE: Tony. Did you know your dad and Miss Phillips are getting married?

[*Silence.* DUDGEON *is stunned*]

BOY [*softly*]: Nah. They didn't say.

[*Pause*]

CLIFFE: I'm sorry.

BOY: Thas all?

CLIFFE: No—

BOY: Can I go now?

SEELEY: He's due back now—

CLIFFE: Yes.

[*The door opens and the* GOVERNOR *enters*]

GOVERNOR: You here, Bob?

CLIFFE: Yes sir. Plus Seeley and Dudgeon. They were just going.

GOVERNOR: Take him back, Mr Seeley.

SEELEY: Sir!

[CLIFFE *offers his hand to* DUDGEON, *who deliberately ignores it.* SEELEY *pushes him out*]

GOVERNOR: What's up?

CLIFFE: You were right.

[*Outside,* DUDGEON *slowly puts his boots on*]

GOVERNOR: He's told you?

CLIFFE: The words in acid.

GOVERNOR: Well done. [*Pause*] Well, what's up?

CLIFFE: He as good as asked me what right I had to . . . question him. He's dead right.

GOVERNOR: You had my permission.

CLIFFE: Sir, when he smashed the ashtray he kept a splinter of glass . . . and he's not to be searched according to your instructions. He might do something.

GOVERNOR: Go out and get drunk. Forget it. You'll make a good doctor one day. But don't try to find a reason for everything.

[*Outside,* DUDGEON *is marched off by* SEELEY. *The maraccas roll as* CLIFFE *packs his bag*]

What're those?

CLIFFE: Maraccas.

GOVERNOR: M—what—ers?

CLIFFE: They're used for rhythm. Try them—go on.

[*He puts them into the* GOVERNOR'*s hands*]

GOVERNOR: What do they test, eh? [*He plays them and produces clumsy rhythms*] Never was much of a hand at music. What do they do?

CLIFFE: Oh—I somehow felt . . . no murderer could have a consistent sense of rhythm.

GOVERNOR: Why not?

CLIFFE: There'd be a break somewhere.

GOVERNOR: Did you try it on big boy?

CLIFFE: Oh yes. He was immaculate. There was no break. He was better than me and ten times better than you. Funny.

GOVERNOR: Are you going to use tomorrow?

CLIFFE: No, I've finished.

[*Fade. Lights up on the cell*]

SEELEY [*off*]: Halt!

[*Sounds of heavy grating being unlocked off-stage.* SEELEY *and* DUDGEON *appear*]

[*Worried*] You all right, kid?

BOY [*toneless*]: Yes . . . sir.

SEELEY: Get in then—and sharpish.

[DUDGEON *enters the cell.* SEELEY *closes it*]

BOY: Here—take this. [*He hands over the sliver of glass through the bars*]

SEELEY: What's this?

BOY: <u>Glass</u>.

SEELEY: Glass?

BOY: It cuts things.

SEELEY: Where did you get it? [*Pause*] I'll have to report this.

BOY: Go on then. [*He turns his back on* SEELEY]

SEELEY [*kind*]: All right kid. You did right. G'night. G'night.

[SEELEY *exits. Offstage we hear the grating clang as it is locked. Silence.* DUDGEON *turns and stares through the bars at the audience. The lights slowly fade*]

THE END

Excursion

(A play for voices)

ALAN PLATER

CAST

NORMAN
TOM
ARTHUR
EDIE
DORIS
TERRY
PETE
SHEILA
BERNARD

Excursion

SCENE: *Inside a football excursion train: an open compartment.*

NORMAN [*to himself, as throughout*]: An excursion train will depart from City Station at 10.35 arriving at 13.45 . . . Returning at 23.43 and arriving back at City Station at 02.56 . . . proving . . . it takes three minutes longer coming back than going . . . Special rate, thirty-five bob return, refreshments will be available on the train—we know what *that* means—boozing and singing, vomiting even, I shouldn't wonder. [*He opens a newspaper*] 'The stage is set for an epic gladitorial contest as the gallant underdogs tackle the Midland giants . . .'

*

Another part of the same carriage.

TOM: '. . . as the gallant underdogs tackle the Midland giants . . .'

ARTHUR: Eh?

TOM: 'tackle the Midland giants . . .'

ARTHUR: By God, they write some stuff, them fellers . . .

TOM: They're all alike. Rubbish. Our Edie likes it . . .

ARTHUR: Doris's the same . . .

TOM: They're all the same . . .

*

On the platform outside.

EDIE: All murders, isn't it?

DORIS: Yes it is, isn't it?

EDIE: Shooting and strangling and goings on, they shouldn't put it in the paper . . .

DORIS: I mean, it's the youngsters, really. Hey [*She points to two teenagers*] look over there!

EDIE [*disapproving*]: I wonder who let them out.

*

Lower down the same platform.

TERRY: Come on, beanbrain, over here . . .

PETE: Shut up!

TERRY: Beanbrain.

PETE: I said beside the bookstall . . .

TERRY: Under the clock, you said. Who wants to buy books?

PETE: And you said . . .

TERRY: I had to go back home for something, that's why I was a bit late . . .

PETE: What you forget? Your head?

TERRY: Here . . . look . . . [*He produces three toilet rolls*]

PETE: Hey, you haven't bought . . . you mad-headed beggar . . .

TERRY: That's right . . .

PETE: You stupid . . .

[*There is a blast on the whistle. Passengers board the train and it sets off*]

*

In the compartment.

NORMAN: Ten and a half minutes late, somebody should start a petition about it. It's a bit misty, is it? Is it mist? More what you'd call smokey, you get to expect it. Let's have a look. They're very quiet. [*He reads from newspaper*] 'Dry with sunny periods, scattered showers later . . . dying out.' Must be smoke then. Not mist. Good. Funny. They're very quiet opposite. Pretty girl. Watch yourself, Norman!

*

The seat opposite to NORMAN's.

SHEILA: Bernard . . .

BERNARD: Yes.

SHEILA: Is it, like, important?

BERNARD: What?

SHEILA: This football match.

BERNARD: It's a cup-tie.

SHEILA: Oh, is it?

BERNARD: Yes.

[*Pause*]

SHEILA: What's that?

BERNARD: They're playing for the F.A. Cup.

SHEILA: You mean if Rovers—is it Rovers? . . .

BERNARD: Rovers, aye . . .

SHEILA: If Rovers win, they get a cup?

BERNARD: No

[*Pause*]

SHEILA: I just thought . . .

BERNARD: If they win, they play somebody else, and then somebody else and . . . like a knockout tournament . . .

SHEILA: Oh, like University Challenge?

BERNARD: Then the two teams left, they play at Wembley, and the winners get the Cup.

SHEILA: Wembley?

BERNARD: It's a big stadium like . . .

SHEILA: I know Wembley. It's where they sing 'Abide With Me'.

BERNARD: Football's the best part really. I mean, that's what it's for . . .

SHEILA: It's a nice hymn, I like it, that and 'Eternal Father'.

*

Elsewhere in the same compartment.

TOM: Remember Wolverhampton, don't you?

ARTHUR: Wolverhampton?

TOM: Don't you?

ARTHUR: I remember Wolverhampton all right.

TOM: What it says here . . . hey, listen. 'Rovers' brilliant left winger, Dave Cummings . . .'

ARTHUR: Let's have a look . . . 'brilliant'?

TOM: Lads in the shop call him Nellie . . .

ARTHUR: Only uses his left leg to stand up on . . .

TOM: I'll tell you something. Dave Cummings, he'd never have got in the team that played at Wolverhampton . . .

ARTHUR: Might have let him pump the ball up, that's all . . .

TOM: Remember that goal Sid Curtis scored? Thirty yards out and . . .

ARTHUR: Who?

TOM: Sid Curtis, blond-headed kid, went to Queen's Park Rangers. The second goal, thirty yards out . . .

ARTHUR: Sid Curtis?

TOM: Went to Queen's Park Rangers.

ARTHUR: Alf Johnson, came from Derby County.

TOM: No, not Alf Johnson . . .

ARTHUR: Second goal at Wolverhampton. Rightfooted, first-timer.

TOM: Sid Curtis couldn't kick with his right foot.

ARTHUR: That's why it was Alf Johnson. Liked his beer.

TOM: Well I'm not going to argue . . .

ARTHUR: No point in arguing . . .

TOM: It was a great goal . . .

ARTHUR: Great goal.

[*Pause*]

TOM: I'll not forget Wolverhampton in a hurry.

*

In the opposite seats.

EDIE: They say it's a lovely shopping centre. Our Joan says . . .

DORIS: I know. Our Albert, the one that had shingles, he was saying, it's noted for woollens . . .

EDIE: Is it really?

DORIS: Woollens, yes . . .

EDIE: Well, most places are noted for something . . .

DORIS: Here it's woollens . . . .

EDIE: Fancy.

DORIS: So when Arthur said about the excursion, I said to myself, well . . .

EDIE: You did right, Doris . . .

DORIS: Like he looked a bit sideways at me but . . .

EDIE: So did Tom. As long as you don't come to the match, he says, you can do what . . . [*Quietly*] what the hell you like.

DORIS: Do you know, I've never heard your Tom swear.

EDIE: This afternoon, it'll be like that. Referees, that's what sets him off mostly. Referees.

DORIS: I don't think Arthur likes them very much either.

EDIE: Do you need any woollens?

DORIS: I don't know. I won't really know till I see some.

*

We have now met everybody. Their voices come and go.

SHEILA: How do you know which is Rovers?

BERNARD: Rovers wear red shirts and white shorts.

SHEILA: I see. [*Pause*] All the time?

BERNARD: How do you mean, all the time?

SHEILA: Every time they have a match?

BERNARD: All teams do, they all wear the same colours for every match, more or less . . .

SHEILA: Bit boring, always wearing the same thing.

BERNARD: They're all fellers. Fellers don't bother about things like that.

SHEILA: What about the other team?

BERNARD: United?

SHEILA: What colours?

BERNARD: Green.

[*Pause*]

SHEILA: Don't much like red and green together. They should never be seen . . . my mam says . . .

*

TERRY: Dave Cummings . . .

PETE: What about him?

TERRY: He's a big nancy.

PETE: Is he heck.

TERRY: He's a bigger one than you and that's saying something.

PETE: Best winger they've got.

TERRY: Our mam could play a better game than him.

PETE: Scored last week.

TERRY: Aye, with his backside.

PETE: Give over.

TERRY: Said in the paper: 'a skilful deflection by Cummings'. You what? Nudged the ball with his bum as it went past.

PETE: You're talking rubbish.

TERRY: He nearly died of fright when it went in. He blushed.

PETE: Rubbish.

TERRY: I'm telling you, he blushed. True as I'm riding this bike. Blushed. I've never seen nowt like it.

PETE: Different match to the one I saw.

TERRY: Only to be expected, you being so thick to begin with . . .

*

NORMAN [*reading*]: 'Rovers main hope rests with unorthodox left-winger, Dave Cummings, approaching the veteran stage but still liable to surprise defenders with . . .' [*Pause*] Veteran? He's only . . . thirty-two. What's that make me, if you're a veteran at thirty-two? Never did like this paper. Pretty full, the train. Should be a good gate. They've brought their wives with them. No place for a woman, a cup-tie. I wouldn't take my wife to a cup-tie. That's . . . if I had a wife. Dave Cummings approaching the veteran stage and he's thirty-two and I'm forty-five and haven't got a wife. But it's no place for a wife, a cup-tie. [*Pause*] Anyhow, he was a bloody awful left-winger when he was twenty-seven.

*

DORIS: Well I remember them pillowslips. Did I tell you about the pillowslips . . .?

EDIE: And anyhow I looked and it said 'special offer' and I thought well, that seems . . .

DORIS: How much did you say?

EDIE: Fourteen and eleven . . .

DORIS: Well, you're bound to, aren't you?

EDIE: Special offer. What I mean is, it *was* special . . .

DORIS: At fourteen and eleven . . .

*

TERRY: Six for a shilling.

PETE: Is that all?

TERRY: Special offer.

PETE: Didn't know you went shopping . . .

TERRY: Getting some bread for the old lady; backhander in it, like. Anyhow, there they were, six for a shilling, row upon row, so I got a packet. Stuck one in the lav, two in the kitchen cupboard, three in my pockets . . .

PETE: Start chucking toilet rolls, they'll have you out the ground.

TERRY: Thirty thousand people watching, who'll know who pelted it? 'Hands up who slung the toilet roll'? Give over . . .

PETE: Barmpot.

TERRY: Anyhow, it's only if Rovers score, and everybody's going to be watching the goal when that happens.

PETE: It won't happen.

TERRY: I'm telling you. Three-one.

PETE: Rubbish.

TERRY: Let's see your money.

PETE: All right then. [*Pause*] How much?

TERRY: A note.

PETE: A quid?

TERRY: I'm not bothered, my money's safe.

[*Pause*]

PETE: Right then.

TERRY: Right then. [*Pause*] Pity about that twirp Cummings being on the left wing.

*

BERNARD: What you thinking about?

SHEILA: You like football, don't you?

BERNARD: Yes.

SHEILA: Funny, isn't it? [*Pause*] I like Gene Pitney.

BERNARD: Do you?

SHEILA: Well you know where you are, don't you? With Gene Pitney, or anybody like that.

BERNARD: What's it got to do with football?

SHEILA: Same as the pictures, you know what's on before you go, you know what it's going to be like. Football, you can't tell.

BERNARD: That's the fun. That's what makes it so exciting.

SHEILA: They might lose.

BERNARD: I know. They'll probably lose today.

SHEILA: If you think that, why did you bother coming?

BERNARD: They might not.

SHEILA: That's why . . . ?

BERNARD: If they win it'll be terrific; I want to see it . . . Rovers only Third Division, and them First Division, you see?

SHEILA: I suppose it's daft really, it's nothing like Gene Pitney at all . . . What's Third Division mean?

*

TOM: I remember. Shot straight at him, didn't he? O'Leary it was, Irish international, shot straight at him . . .

ARTHUR: No, he had to move to his left . . .

TOM: Hardly.

ARTHUR: At Wolverhampton you're talking about?

TOM: That's right, just before half-time it was . . .

ARTHUR: Moved to his left . . .

TOM: I don't want to argue but . . .

ARTHUR: I'm not sure he didn't dive.

TOM: He definitely didn't dive.

*

NORMAN [*reading*]: 'Rovers are a well-known cup-fighting side, best remembered for their two-nil win over Wolverhampton Wanderers in the fourth round of the Cup fifteen years ago . . .' [*Pause*] Fifteen years ago? Can't be fifteen. There was the Festival of Britain in 1951 and then . . . yes, fifteen years. [*Pause*] Fifteen years. It's a long time from one bit of glory to the next.

*

ARTHUR: And then they got knocked out next round. Played like girls.

TOM: At home, an' all.

ARTHUR: Right let-down was that.

TOM: Swindon Town.

ARTHUR: Eh?

TOM: Swindon Town.

[*Pause*]

ARTHUR: Darlington.

TOM: Darlington?

ARTHUR: Darlington.

[*Pause*]

TOM: Funny. [*Pause*] I just have a kind of sensation, you know, it might have been Crewe Alexandra.

*

NORMAN: Three miles to the station it said, near that signal box . . . Five minutes. If we were going sixty miles an hour it'd be three minutes. A mile a minute. But we're not. Not even thirty miles an hour now . . . very slowly, you could say. Signals it'll be. I'll put my coat on all the same.

*

SHEILA: We'll have to stand up?

BERNARD: I thought you knew . . .

SHEILA: I thought there'd be sitting down . . .

BERNARD: There is, but you've got to get tickets and . . . costs a bit . . .

SHEILA: How long for?

BERNARD: Couple of hours.

SHEILA: Just in case they win.

*

TERRY: Hey, beanbrain!

PETE: What?

TERRY: You carry that one.

PETE: Get knotted.

TERRY: Go on. Can't have them all under my coat, I look seven months gone . . .

*

NORMAN: You can never tell . . . it could be like Wolverhampton again.

*

TOM: Just hope for the best.

ARTHUR: All you can do.

*

SHEILA: I hope it doesn't rain.

BERNARD: Doesn't rain at football matches.

SHEILA: But if it does . . .

BERNARD: Get wet.

*

EDIE: Have you got your purse, love?

DORIS: Yes. I brought a rain hat. Did you?

EDIE: I've got a scarf I can use.

*

NORMAN: And please, Lord, make Dave Cummings have one of his good days.

[*The train draws to a halt at the station. Then silence*]

We're here.

*

Suddenly, there is noise and activity. We are at the match.

NORMAN: Good crowd. Lot of Rovers people here. If it wasn't for this chap in front I'd have another sandwich—only . . . he wouldn't want tomato down his neck. And I think he's one of theirs . . .

*

TOM: All right, are you?

ARTHUR: Aye, I'm all right, are you all right?

TOM: Aye, I'm all right.

ARTHUR: That's all right then.

TOM: Must be forty thousand here, more than Wolverhampton.

ARTHUR: Never in the world.

*

BERNARD: You'll be all right once they get started.

SHEILA: I must be a bit simple . . .

BERNARD: What for?

SHEILA: Like if I can't see now, how's it all going to change? Will they all go home or something?

*

TERRY: I can see smashing, can you?

PETE: All right, I'll manage.

TERRY: Good lobbing distance.

PETE: There's a lot of coppers round the pitch.

TERRY: Unruly elements in the crowd, that's all they're bothered about.

PETE: Like you.

TERRY: I'm not unruly, just enthusiastic.

*

In a department store.

EDIE [*to assistant*]: Thank you very much.

DORIS: Ask her about the woollens.

EDIE: Where's your wool department please?

*

At the match.

NORMAN: Here they come.

TERRY [*shouting*]: Come on Rovers, you great daft twits!

TOM [*quietly*]: Right lads, let's be having you.

PETE [*yelling*]: Come on Rovers, you useless shower!

ARTHUR: Take it steady, nice and steady.

SHEILA: I can't see.

BERNARD: Rovers have come out.

[*The shouts fade into the background as* NORMAN *speaks*]

NORMAN: Trotting out, muscular, confident, on to the field. Limbering up, sprinting, kicking, heading, rolling their sleeves up. They always look good *before* the match. Look at Dave Cummings, shooting in. Traps the ball like Matthews, smooth and easy; two strides, then thrashes it into the net like Bobby Charlton, younger of the famous footballing brothers from Ashington, Northumberland. Always looks good, Cummings, when he's practising. Hasn't scored in a match proper for two and a half months.

*

TOM: We've won the toss.

ARTHUR: Happen it's the only thing we *will* win.

TOM: I don't know so much. Remember what happened at . . .

ARTHUR: I know, I know . . .

*

SHEILA: Did you say that's us in red?

BERNARD: In red, yes.

SHEILA: They're prettier than the others.

*

TERRY: Come on then Rovers, stand on them.

PETE: Get stuck in.

TERRY: Anything above grass.

PETE: They can't run without legs.

TERRY: No messing, get stuck in.

[*There is a blast on a whistle*]

*

NORMAN: And straight from the kick-off, Rovers are defending. Not muscular any more, not confident any more. Tough, dogged, chasing everything, but the green shirts keep swarming back . . . and their right-winger gets the ball and looks dangerous so two Rovers players trip him up at the same time because they can't stop him any other way . . .

*

TERRY: He's given a free kick. He never touched him.

PETE: Paid fifty thousand pounds for him, they did. Get stuck in!

TERRY: Wouldn't give fifty thousand washers for him. Right pansy.

*

SHEILA: He's got nice fair hair.

BERNARD: You what?

SHEILA: He's got nice hair.

BERNARD: Can't possibly have, he's on their side.

*

TOM: Struggling a bit, Arthur.

ARTHUR: Aye, just a bit.

TOM: Hey, look at that.

ARTHUR: Bit hasty, that.

*

TERRY: Send him off.

PETE: Send him off.

TERRY: Dirty swine.

PETE: What did he do?

TERRY: I didn't see.

*

TOM: Real cup-tie stuff.

ARTHUR: Rough as hell.

TOM: First-time tackling, straight in, bang.

ARTHUR: Hard luck if you get in the way.

TOM: It's grand to watch.

*

NORMAN: Twenty-five minutes gone and Rovers beginning to attack. Not really dangerous, more what you'd call hopeful. Optimistic. Hit hard and hope. Up and under. Kick and rush. Thump it down the middle and run like hell. Then, suddenly, with a rush of blood to the head, somebody rolls the ball neatly, quietly along the ground to Dave Cummings on the wing.

[*The crowd gets excited*]

TOM: Fancy giving it to him.

ARTHUR: Get a move on with it . . .

TOM: Standing there gawping . . .

ARTHUR: Fannying about.

*

TERRY: He's just stood there.

PETE: Get rid of it.

TERRY: Boot it.

*

TOM: Push it down the wing.

ARTHUR: Centre forward's waiting for the pass.

TOM: He's going to shoot.

*

TERRY: Shooting from right out there . . .

PETE: The nit, the steaming Scottish nit!

[*A sudden silence*]

*

NORMAN [*quietly*]: And Cummings shoots, from thirty yards, and he scores.

*

In the shop.

EDIE: Which do you like best?

DORIS: I like the beige, I think.

EDIE: That fawn's nice.

DORIS: That's a pretty one, what is it?

EDIE: Terra cotta it says on it.

*

At the match.

TOM: What a lovely goal.

ARTHUR: Goalie never saw it.

TOM: Like a flaming rocket.

ARTHUR: With his wrong foot.

*

BERNARD: Did you see it? Did you see it?

SHEILA: That was a goal wasn't it?

BERNARD: A beauty.

SHEILA: Was that our side? Was it the red ones?

*

TERRY: Cummings, you're the greatest.

PETE: He's the greatest all right.

TERRY: Here we go.

PETE: Hey stoppit!

TERRY: We've scored a bloody goal, man, what do you expect me to do? . . . Come on the lads . . . ! [TERRY *throws his toilet roll*]

*

NORMAN: And a bit of trouble behind one of the goals, kids throwing toilet rolls. Policemen moving in. Oh dear, oh dear, what a pity, what a pity. A lovely goal though. Dave Cummings, you'd have thought he was practising. [*Blast on whistle*] Half time.

*

In a café.

EDIE: Nice cup of tea.

DORIS: Very nice.

[*Pause*]

EDIE: It's a nice colour.

DORIS: What colour did she say it was?

EDIE: Cinnamon.

DORIS: Cinnamon.

EDIE: Dirty brown I'd call it.

*

A street outside the football ground.

TERRY: Beanbrain.

PETE: You're the beanbrain.

TERRY: It was you saying 'It wasn't us, it wasn't us'. He's bound to be suspicious, isn't he?

PETE: I didn't pelt the flaming thing.

TERRY: That's got nowt to do with it.

PETE: Course it has.

TERRY: Flaming hasn't.

PETE: We're watching the second half out here in the street, right?

TERRY: What of it?

PETE: If you hadn't slung the toilet roll, we'd still be inside.

TERRY: It's not a bad street.

[*Blast on whistle*]

*

At the match.

TOM: I fancy 'em you know, Arthur.

ARTHUR: It's early days but it could be . . . another Wolverhampton.

TOM: Another Wolverhampton.

ARTHUR: By heck. We've waited years.

TOM: Years and years.

*

NORMAN: History might repeat itself. Rovers holding out

with something to spare, only occasionally resorting to shirt-pulling, ankle-tapping and elbow-digging. Even then, they're more sinned against than sinning. It's United that's getting desperate now.

*

SHEILA: Why did the police do that?

BERNARD: Because they threw a toilet roll.

SHEILA: Why did they throw it?

BERNARD: Cause Rovers scored. They were happy about it.

SHEILA: Are you not allowed to be happy?

BERNARD: Only according to the rules.

SHEILA: Is it all right shouting what that fella was shouting?

BERNARD: What was he shouting?

SHEILA: I'll whisper.

*

TOM: Look at that. Lovely play, Dave.

ARTHUR: Playing well, is Cummings.

TOM: He's a good lad, good ball player, that's the thing.

ARTHUR: Usually are, from Scotland.

*

NORMAN: Dave Cummings, the hero of Rovers. One week in ten they love him more than The Beatles or The Queen. The rest of the time he's a cross between Charlie Drake and Mussolini. He's playing a lovely game. They all are, all playing a lovely game, better even than they did that day at Wolverhampton. [*Pause*] Until . . . until suddenly the centre half slips, and the centre-forward gets the ball and he's clean through, churning through the middle towards the goal, and only Rovers' goalkeeper to beat . . . just the two of them and everything seems to stop.

*

In a street.

EDIE: Where did we say we'd meet them?

DORIS: Town Hall steps.

EDIE: Along this way I think . . .

DORIS: We must have walked miles.

*

At the match.

NORMAN: A goal!

*

In the street.

TERRY: It's a goal!

PETE: One-all.

TERRY: Rovers have scored again, two-nil . . .

PETE: One-all . . .

*

At the match.

TOM: One-all.

ARTHUR: Would you credit it.

TOM: One-all. One flaming all.

*

SHEILA: Bernard . . .

BERNARD: What?

SHEILA: What's the matter?

BERNARD: What's the matter? What's the matter? Don't you know?

SHEILA: I can tell there's something wrong . . .

*

NORMAN: United equalise. Three minutes to go and they equalise. Five thousand men, women and children want to cry. It's in the nature of a betrayal . . . like biting into a soft centre only to find caramel.

[*The final whistle blows*]

It's all over.

*

ARTHUR: It's a good job I left the dog at home.

TOM: Ours an' all.

ARTHUR: I'd boot it over yon stand.

*

BERNARD: There was only three minutes to go.

SHEILA: That's no excuse for language like that . . .

BERNARD: Yes it is . . .

SHEILA: If that's what football matches do . . .

BERNARD: Well they do! That's what football matches do!

*

In the street.

TERRY: One-all.

PETE: I told you.

TERRY: Hard luck though, wasn't it?

PETE: We didn't see half of it, we don't know.

TERRY: Must have been hard luck. If it'd been ten-one, it'd still be hard luck.

PETE: You're a nut-case.

TERRY: Never mind. Half an hour and the pubs are open.

*

NORMAN: And now we've all got to find something to do until 23.43 . . . twenty to midnight . . . wine, women and song. Ha ha. Have to find a café, all my sandwiches have gone soggy.

*

EDIE: You'll be able to tell by their faces.

DORIS: They're taking their time.

EDIE: You should see him come in when they've lost. Slams the door, chucks his cap in the corner, dog goes under a chair . . .

EDIE: Is that them?

DORIS: Where?

EDIE: That's them. Tom looks happy enough. Arthur looks as if he's had a nasty accident.

DORIS: Must have been a draw then.

*

In a pub. PETE & TERRY *are reading a newspaper.*

TERRY: There's wrestling.

PETE: Don't be stupid.

TERRY: Here we are: the Majestic. Sounds like the place . . .

PETE: Eight o'clock.

TERRY: That's in about . . . six pints from now . . .

PETE: I've still got that other toilet roll.

TERRY: Hang on to it.

PETE: What for?

TERRY: You might want to wipe your nose.

*

In a Chinese restaurant.

NORMAN: Sweet and sour king prawns with boiled rice or

chips . . . What's this one? Green dragon special with bamboo shoots, bean sprouts, egg, noodles. Don't fancy that. Here we are . . . haddock, peas and chips. I wonder what *they're* having?

*

DORIS: Our Natalie was telling me, she'd had something nice in one of these places. Now what was it?

TOM: Curried hedge clippings.

ARTHUR: There's some right stuff down here, by heck.

EDIE: You'll like it.

TOM: Aye.

ARTHUR: Aye.

DORIS: What you having then?

EDIE: I don't know. What you having?

DORIS: What you having Arthur?

ARTHUR: What you having Tom?

TOM: I'll have what Edie has.

EDIE: I'm not all that hungry, we had them scones.

TOM: All right then, I'll have a Green Dragon special, as long as there's not too many dragons in it.

*

Outside a cinema.

BERNARD: It's all right, the queue's moving.

SHEILA: About time.

BERNARD: There's no queue at that one down the street.

SHEILA: Don't want to go there, it's an Italian film.

BERNARD: What about it?

SHEILA: Well it'll be in Italian, won't it?

BERNARD: I should think so.

SHEILA: They always are, I saw one on the telly.

BERNARD: Do you like Charlton Heston?

SHEILA: He's all right.

BERNARD: You know where you are with him, any road.

SHEILA: Oh yes.

BERNARD: Not like football.

SHEILA: Nothing to do with football.

*

In the restaurant.

DORIS: Edie got some wool.

TOM: Good. She got some wool, Arthur.

ARTHUR: Oh aye. Good.

EDIE: Ask me what colour.

TOM: Oh aye . . . any special colour?

EDIE: Cinnamon.

[*Pause*]

TOM: Cinnamon?

EDIE: That's its name.

TOM: More like a dirty brown to me.

EDIE: It was very reasonable. Apparently it's noted for wool . . .

TOM: Cinnamon?

ARTHUR: When I was a lad, I remember we used to smoke cinnamon.

TOM: That's right, I remember.

ARTHUR: I don't remember knitting any.

EDIE [*noticing* NORMAN]: He was on the train, him that just went out.

*

In the street.

NORMAN: Is it coming on to rain? No. Just thought, for a minute. Four hours yet. [*Pause*] Pictures? What's this one . . . Italian . . . let's see the pictures . . . [*Reacts*] Oh dear it's one of those ones . . . So what's it matter, you're a long way from home . . . Walking up and asking for the tickets, that's the hard part . . . There's one further along . . . Bible epic. Bit of a queue though. Best . . . walk about a bit . . . think about it . . . plenty time.

*

Inside the cinema.

BERNARD: Are you all right?

SHEILA: Yes thanks. [*Pause*] It's warm. I can see everything. I've got an ice-cream.

BERNARD: Same here.

SHEILA: Guess what it's better than.

*

In the street.

NORMAN: Summarising then, we would seem to have, on the one hand . . . Charlton Heston in *Second Book of Kings* . . . on the other hand, or, if you prefer it, at the dark end of the street . . . *Sweet Passion in the Ricefields* with subtitles . . . It isn't easy, it isn't easy at all . . .

*

In the restaurant.

EDIE: How much longer are you going to be?

TOM: Plenty time.

DORIS: Just 'cause they found out it had a licence . . .

TOM: Well Edie doesn't like pubs.

ARTHUR: It's a fair drop of brown, this, for bottled stuff.

EDIE: There's the bill.

TOM: Two pound three and six . . .

ARTHUR: There's a place near the works, you can get hot pie, peas and chips for half a crown, and that includes your bread-and-butter and tea . . .

EDIE: We're having a day out, it doesn't matter.

DORIS: If Rovers had won, it wouldn't have mattered.

ARTHUR: I'm not so sure that goal they got wasn't offside, Tom.

TOM: I thought so at the time.

EDIE: Forget about football for five minutes . . .

TOM: Oh. We'll split this, Arthur . . . Nice . . . nice bit of wool that was you bought, love.

*

In the dance hall.

TERRY: It's a right place this, isn't it?

PETE: Like a battlefield, isn't it?

TERRY: Well, it's Saturday night, they're all looking for it. [*Pause*] Well. No time to waste.

PETE: Off are you?

TERRY: Redhead. If we're leaving at eleven I'll have to be quick out the traps.

PETE: All the best.

TERRY: I'll be all right, don't worry, kid.

*

In the street.

NORMAN: *Sweet Passion in the Ricefields* . . . seats in all parts . . . it's a woman in the paybox. I don't think I could look her in the eyes . . . Hey, there's a second feature . . . *Naked and Unashamed,* now showing. [*Pause*] *Second Book of Kings.*

*

In the cinema.

SHEILA: I'm glad you're enjoying it. I like biblical films.

BERNARD: Yes. [*Pause*] Sheila . . .

SHEILA: Yes.

BERNARD: Sorry but . . . I've got cramp in my arm.

SHEILA: Oh have you . . . there . . .

BERNARD [*groans*]: Shoots right through you, right past my shoulder.

VOICE: Shhh!

*

In the street.

NORMAN: No point in going in now, two thirds the way through the film, last performance. [*Sighs*] Half past nine. Two hours. If I walk very slowly to the station, then have a cup of tea there, buy a paper. Then the train might be there and I could sit on it. In it. That's the best plan. A slow walk.

*

In the dance hall.

TERRY: Now then kid.

PETE: Hallo Terry, I thought you'd got fixed up.

TERRY: She's got a fella here.

PETE: Didn't you sort him out?

TERRY: He was about seven foot six.

PETE: Aim low.

TERRY: And he'd got about nine mates, and they were all seven foot six an' all . . .

PETE: Where you going?

TERRY: Up on the balcony. [*They move up*]

PETE: What you going to do? Hey, where do you get that from? [*The toilet roll*]

TERRY: Your coat in the cloakroom.

PETE: You can't throw that in here . . .

TERRY: Where is he?

PETE: Terry, you're a raving lunatic . . .

TERRY: That's right. There he is, by hell, he's a good target, being so tall . . .

PETE: I'm off.

TERRY: Here we go . . . [*Pause*] Good kid Terry, a direct hit. Poleaxed the bastard.

*

In the street.

TOM: Station's this way.

EDIE: Are you sure?

DORIS: There's the Town Hall.

ARTHUR: General Post Office.

EDIE: We've been calling it the Town Hall.

ARTHUR: General Post Office.

TOM: Ministry of Social Security. And the station's up that way.

*

BERNARD: He played a storming game though.

SHEILA: What?

BERNARD: Dave Cummings.

SHEILA: I think Charlton Heston's very good.

BERNARD: Yes, he is. Very good. [*Pause*] Did you want to get a bus to the station?

SHEILA: I think I'd rather walk.

BERNARD: I'd rather walk as well.

SHEILA: Best thing if we walk then.

*

PETE: Which way's the station?

TERRY: God knows. Could be straight up for all I know.

PETE: You're a dope.

TERRY: Never dull though, is it kid?

PETE: Getting us slung out the dance and the football match, it's not bad.

TERRY: Didn't half fetch him a crack, it did, the twit.

PETE: Wonder he didn't fetch you one.

TERRY: Wasn't watching was he?

PETE: That bouncer was watching though, wasn't he?

TERRY: He was a big kid wasn't he? Legs like tree trunks.

PETE: Where's the flaming station?

TERRY: I haven't got it.

PETE: If we miss the train . . .

TERRY: If we miss it, at least we won't get slung off it.

*

Inside the train.

NORMAN: Departing at 23.43 and arriving at City Station at 02.56 . . . Still a bit worried by the three minutes difference between coming and going . . .

*

EDIE: I'm tired.

DORIS: Our Tony was going to leave our electric blanket on.

EDIE: I'll have my bottle. I like my bottle . . .

TOM: Could have been, you know.

ARTHUR: Could very easily have been.

TOM: Just for that goal three minutes from the end . . .

ARTHUR: An offside goal.

TOM: And it would have been another Wolverhampton.

*

SHEILA: You said it was one goal each.

BERNARD: Yes.

SHEILA: And you get a goal for kicking it between them posts.

BERNARD: Yes.

SHEILA: I saw them kick it between the posts three times.

BERNARD: They got one, it was disallowed. Somebody fouled.

SHEILA: Is that like cheating? That feller standing behind me called the referee that . . . that word . . .

BERNARD: He did, didn't he?

SHEILA: What's it mean? That word? Exactly what does it mean?

[*There is a blast on a whistle*]

*

NORMAN: 23.43 and away . . . and two lads sprinting down the platform. It shouldn't be allowed.

[TERRY & PETE *leap on the train as it is moving*]

*

TERRY [*breathless*]: Bloodyell . . .

PETE: It's great going away with you.

TERRY: That's why I'm so popular.

PETE: Slung out of everywhere.

TERRY: We're on our way home.

PETE: You're not fit to be out on your own!

TERRY: That's why I brought you with me.

*

TOM: Coming back from Wolverhampton . . .

ARTHUR: Played cards all the way . . .

TOM: Solo.

ARTHUR: Poker.

TOM: I'm going to say it was solo.

ARTHUR: I've a recollection it was three card brag.

EDIE: They're funny, aren't they?

DORIS: They're funny all right.

EDIE: I mean. They just live from one football match to the next. Keeps them going, somehow.

*

SHEILA: Bernard love . . .

BERNARD: Yes?

SHEILA: I think another time . . . you go on your own to football matches . . . I think I'm wasted on a football match.

BERNARD: We'll go some other place next time.

SHEILA: I'd like that. [*Pause*] I'll have to tell George.

BERNARD: George?

SHEILA: Just this lad, don't worry about it . . . I'll sort it out.

BERNARD: What lad?

SHEILA: Shhhh!

∗

NORMAN: The Saturday Green 'Un . . . 'Gallant Rovers surprise over-confident United. Late equaliser prevents sensational victory . . .' It seems about a million years ago.

∗

TOM: Funny, the women, they just live from one special offer to the next . . .

ARTHUR: Aye, I've noticed. It's only shop windows keeps them going.

EDIE: Doris . . . did you see them lengths of curtain material . . . [*But* DORIS *is asleep*] She's asleep.

∗

BERNARD: Sheila . . . who is he? [*But* SHEILA *is asleep*] Asleep.

∗

TERRY: Hey Pete . . . ?

PETE [*sleepily*]: Shuttup.

TERRY: Party on tomorrow night. Are you coming?

PETE: Shut up.

TERRY: I'll come round in the morning, fix it up.

PETE: Shut up.

TERRY: Right then. I'll go see what's doing in the buffet car. Coming?

PETE: Shut up. No I am not. And you haven't got any money.

TERRY: Aye. [*Pause*] Good night then.

*

TOM: Lovely goal.

ARTHUR: Cummings?

TOM: Aye.

ARTHUR: Nice pass from McDonald.

TOM: Murphy. I've a feeling it was Murphy.

[*Pause*]

ARTHUR: Hang on. I think you're right. I think it was Murphy.

TOM: Eh?

ARTHUR: My mistake.

[*Pause*]

TOM: Are you sure it was Murphy?

*

NORMAN: Tomorrow, it'll be over, barring the Sunday papers. Over now really, till the replay next Wednesday. From one to the next to the next. It's a good trip, a football trip, when you win. When you lose, it's a hell of a long way back. When you draw . . . it's sort of ordinary, sort of grey. Not black and not white. Rovers, they have more black than white, on the whole. Mostly it's grey, just dull grey and ordinary. [*Pause*] But we keep on watching, keep on waiting . . . waiting for the white. If you don't keep on going, you might miss it. [*Pause*] And there's nothing worse than knowing it's been . . . and knowing you've missed it.

[*The train speeds on into the night*]

THE END

A Dead Liberty

ALAN GOSLING

CAST

JACK FLINT
GINNY FLINT
BROTHER
DOCTOR

All applications to perform this play, whether by amateurs or professionals, should be made to Harvey Unna Ltd, 14 Beaumont Mews, Marylebone High Street, London W1

A Dead Liberty

SCENE: *A house, near Clapham Junction. The curtain rises to discover* GINNY FLINT *hunched on her pouffe by the fire. Her living room is tidy, but everything is old and dingy. A door at the right opens into what would be the little hallway. At the left is a kitchen alcove, with a wash boiler jammed under the tiny draining board. The rooms form a wedge shape because the house is on a corner. The wallpaper is tanned with smoke.* GINNY *wears tea-coloured clothes so that she blends in. The overmantel is stuffed with bills and final demands, giving the impression that everything is paid for at the last moment on borrowed money.*

The front door slams [off]. GINNY *jumps up and turns up the gas under the kettle.* FLINT *enters ponderously in his working clothes. He takes off his jacket, extending it grandly, for he has had a couple on the way home, and he sings as she shuffles by, taking it to hang it up. He is obviously master in this house.*

Time: the present.

FLINT [*sings*]: 'She was standin' in the guttah! Sellin' matches by the box!' [*Peering*] What are you looking so flamin' happy about then?

[GINNY *wrings her hands miserably and goes all the way back to the kitchen to get the cups out*]

GINNY: I don't like to tell yer!

FLINT [*sitting in his great chair*]: Oh I see it . . . it's goin' to be mystery half hour now . . .

GINNY: Well he's dead.

FLINT: Where?

GINNY: In his bed.

FLINT: Who is?

GINNY: Fred.

FLINT: Which Fred?

GINNY: *Our* Fred.

FLINT: In his bed?

GINNY: Like I said.

FLINT [*rising*]: Gawd 'elpus.

GINNY [*bringing cups in*]: I dittn't like to tell you.

[*He gets up, and looks at the place above the fire where* FRED *would be lying*]

FLINT: I bet he ain't.

GINNY: I bet he is!

[*An express train roars by outside and they both pause, trembling with the vibrations. An ornament falls down*]

FLINT [*looking at window*]: Golden Arrer!

GINNY [*looking at clock*]: Dead on time too.

FLINT: There's anuvver ornament busted!

GINNY: It's the rotten vibrations! They're shaking this rotten house to bits!

FLINT: Give over then.

GINNY: It's the rott'nest house in the road!

FLINT: Well you wanna get the ornament swep' up then, make it a bit tidier! And get that tea made!

[*He sits again while she goes out to make it*]

GINNY: I bin sittin' tremblin'.

FLINT: Go on?

GINNY: Well, I'm frightened about him! [*Pointing upward*]

FLINT: Oh yuh?

GINNY: Well, ain't you scared?

FLINT: If he was dead I would be.

GINNY: He is Jack. Honest.

FLINT: Listen. He was sitting up that table at half past six! Eatin' a kipper out of a plastic bag!

GINNY: I never said he wasn't!

FLINT: And I'll tell YOU sunnink! He scoffed the last of the swiss roll while you was out the back!

GINNY: I said he could.

FLINT [*pointing to the television*]: You bin squintin' at *that* fing again, aincher? You've got mixed up.

GINNY: I just had it on for the hosspiddle story!

FLINT [*disgustedly*]: Don' gimme that! You've had it on all night. You never have it off.

GINNY [*bringing in tea things*]: You never believe what I tell you.

E

FLINT: Telly *mad*. [*He goes and throws open the door into the hallway and bawls*] Cupper tea dahn here Mister Merit!

[*A long silence*]

GINNY: There you are, he's dead.

FLINT [*triumphantly*]: Jus' because he don' wanna cup of tea?

GINNY: Well run up and take a shufti at him then!

FLINT: Run up and . . . Have you gorn out of your mind?

GINNY: You'll see for yourself.

FLINT: Listen mate. I goes up them stairs once at night, and comes dahn once in the mornin'. Is that correct?

GINNY: Yes Jack.

FLINT: Well I ain't changin' my habits for one lousy lodger! Bang on the ceilin' with the broom, that always flushes him aht. And pour that tea out, I'm parched.

GINNY: You bin drinkin' all evening!

FLINT [*blandly*]: That's right. Roll us a fag.

GINNY [*as she concentrates on this, under the light in the centre*]: You see, after you wen' out, he started looking dicky.

FLINT: I shouldn't wonder, after kippers and swiss roll!

GINNY: Then he kep' putting his hand over his mouth and sayin' 'Excuse me'—so I offered him a couple of bladder pills!

FLINT: Where'd you get them from?

GINNY: The sideboard. They're what me Dad useta take.

FLINT: But he's bin dead years! Them pills must be rock 'ard. No wonder he's snuffed it!

GINNY: But he never took em'! He said he dittn't want 'em!

FLINT: Don't blame him. You gunna pour that tea then?

GINNY: I ain't finished this fag yet.

FLINT: Well come on then gel. You know I like a cuppa tea and a good cough in the warm, before I go up . . .

[*She finishes the cigarette and takes it over and puts it in his mouth. He raises his eyebrows. She gets the matches off the shelf and lights his cigarette and he inhales deeply then bends over and starts to cough quietly, looking at her like a beaten dog. She takes this opportunity to get her story in as quickly as she can*]

GINNY: He went sorta all horrible and green and he starts tremblin' and he dragged hisself to the doorway. Then he broke out in sweat. 'I don't feel so good,' he said. 'Oh don't you?' I said.

[FLINT's *cough breaks out into a rapid bark, then fades*]

FLINT: Carry on dear.

GINNY: Then his face flushed up purple and he hung on the door, you see, and I thought 'hallo'—and he shut down his eyelids and went back white again, like sort of all white as a sheet, then he said, 'I think I'll lay down for five minutes,' so I said, 'ye-es!'

FLINT: Tea's gettin' cold.

GINNY: Ooh yeh! [*Starting to pour*]

FLINT: He really done all that did he? All that changin' colour every five seconds . . .

GINNY: True!

FLINT: He'd make a fortune, up the Junction, on a Saturday mornin' wouldn't he? Changin' colours like that!

GINNY: You don't believe a word I'm saying, do you?

FLINT: I believe yer!

GINNY: Do yer?

FLINT [*turning away to hide his grin*]: I read abaht it in the Sunday Pic. It's sunnink to do with the way they smoke kippers these days.

GINNY: Ooh-er!

FLINT: Yeh, you keep gettin hot and cold flushes and your face goes all colours . . .

GINNY: Well he did!

FLINT [*mischievously*]: Did he bust into flames after that and shoot up through the ceiling?

GINNY: Course not!

FLINT: Oh . . . it ain't the same disease what I read about . . .

GINNY: You're muckin' about Jack!

FLINT: Well of course I am. [*Drinking his tea down in one great gulp after another*] You daft mare. G'night.

[*He goes to the door, ready to get up to bed. His back aches and he stops to rub it. She gets her coat and starts to put it on*]

GINNY: I'm gunna run next door and git Rene!

FLINT: Oy!

GINNY: Well I want to be sure whether he is dead or not!

FLINT: Aaaaah, you ain't sure now?

GINNY: Well, y'see I put a mirror in front of his nose . . . this was after . . . when he was in bed . . . and it never steamed up . . . so I felt his pulse! Like, on his wrist! Then I give him a really hard good shake. [*Acting this most hysterically*] 'There's some tea in the pot if you wanna cup Mister Merit!!'

FLINT: Git that coat off. I'll look in on him on my way up.

[*Whistling mournfully, he goes out and is heard mounting the stairs. She flits over to sweep up the broken ornament. She kneels upright*]

GINNY [*to herself*]: I'm sure he is.

[JACK FLINT *clatters down the stairs, grabs his coat and puts it on, then takes it straight off again. He drops it on the floor. She leaps up and follows three inches behind him as he takes a drink of water, then she follows him round as he rummages in the sideboard for a cigarette, then she gets one from her handbag and puts it in his mouth and lights it up for him. He stands beside her, hugely blowing a vast cloud of smoke. He shifts his feet about aimlessly, registering amazement and disgust. She hovers near him waiting for his deliberation. He flicks ash off his cigarette*]

FLINT: Morry-bund.

GINNY: I said he was.

FLINT: Did you?

GINNY: When you COME IN!

FLINT: I recklect, you said you wasn't sure!

GINNY: I said, 'Fred's dead,' I said . . .

FLINT: Well it don't matter what you said, he's dead! Stick to the *gist* of it!

[*She rises quickly, doing a triumphant lap round the table, lifting his coat off the floor and bringing it round, opening it ready to help him on with it*]

GINNY: Well, you gotta do sunnink now!

FLINT: Such as what?

GINNY: You gotta put your coat on and get out and go down the road and . . .

FLINT: Bury him?

[*Pause*]

GINNY: No, well uh . . .

FLINT [*triumphantly*]: Aaaaaaaah! Hang me coat up. Make some more tea. Let *me* do the thinking Ginny . . . Please . . .

GINNY: All right Jack . . .

FLINT: There are certain things we have gotta do. Action is wanted at this stage! Get the kettle on.

[*She hurries to do this brightly*]

GINNY: I feel more settled in me mind now Jack . . . you know . . . now we're going to DO sunnink . . . I was real bad, shocked . . . you know . . .

FLINT [*ponderously*]: It's quite a disturbin' psychliggickal experience seeing a—dead party. Specially if you're sensitive . . .

GINNY: Yes Jack . . .

FLINT: Which you *ain't*, of course.

GINNY [*hardly having heard*]: No Jack . . .

[*She hums and lahs 'Abide with me' as she does a contented lap round the table, to rinse the crocks.* FLINT *has gone wooden in thought. He jerks*]

FLINT: Inform the reequisite authorities! That'll be the strength of it Ginny! Am I right or wrong?

GINNY [*at sink now*]: Yes Jack.

FLINT: C'mere!

[*He walks with dignity to the upright chair at the table and sits. As she comes in, he points to the seat opposite. She goes to sit, and just, as her bottom barely hits the seat . . .*]

The book!

GINNY [*rising again*]: What book?

[*They gaze around the cluttered bookless room thoughtfully*]

FLINT: The book what Teddy borrowed from the library about ten years ago . . .

GINNY [*realising*]: Oh, yes . . . THE book . . .

[*She goes round the table, anti-clockwise again, confusedly, looking up in the air, everywhere, in a vague hope of it springing from somewhere, and goes round the back of the table, passing through to the kitchen, coming to a halt by the draining board, under which is the wash-boiler. She peers downward and straightens up with a simple smile of pleasure*]

GINNY: I stuck it under the washing machine!

FLINT: Typical.

GINNY: The wheel come off. [*Delighted to relate this item*] 'Ere, the wheel come off you see . . . and I looked, in the book, to see if it said how to fix it. Well I couldn't find nuthink about it so—

FLINT [*tiredly*]: You stuck it where the wheel useta be. [*Bitterly*] Just git it!

[*She tugs insipidly*]

GINNY: Ooohugh . . .

FLINT: What're you poncin abaht at, out there . . . ?

[*He has risen on the last of this, crossing to her, and grabs her backside in one hand as she is bent still tugging, and pulls her out of the way. Then he stands back and squints at the problem with the eye of a skilled warehouse-humper. He grips the machine and eases it out smoothly. The draining board comes down in a shower of crockery*]

GINNY: The struts've rusted!

FLINT [*bawls*]: Oy!!

[*He kicks the crocks into a tidier collation and goes into the living room and sits, breathing heavily*]

FLINT [*strainedly*]: Ginny, you must learn to cut out the trivillarities . . . I MEAN, here we are in the middle of life and death. And you go on about a couple of rusted struts. [*Opening book*] You are a rill help. [*Sniffing book*] This book's gorn rotten, here get a whiff of that odour . . .

GINNY [*sniffing*]: Poooo!

FLINT [*thumbing over pages*]: Ah!

[*He makes a number of signalling gestures with both arms as he squints at the book. She watches uncomprehendingly*]

GINNY: What's all that then Jack?

FLINT: Semaphore. Used to do that when I was a kid. [*Thumbing over pages*] Here we are! [*Peering*] This print ennarf tiny. Git your Dad's old glasses.

[*She gets them from a drawer and hands them to him. He puts them on. They look like sunglasses*]

GINNY: The lens are all gummed up with muck!

FLINT: Well you wanna bung a wet rag over them once in a way out of respect for your dad then. Here you read it. [*He rises, standing at ease, bowing his head to listen*]

GINNY [*reading*]: The evarage ex—expectoration of life of man in the British Isles is fifty-eight and a half years . . .

FLINT [*pointing*]: How old was *he*?

GINNY: Said he was sixty-three.

FLINT: Ah well . . . he's had a pretty good run then, according to the form they give here! Do it say anything about funerals?

GINNY [*finding place*]: Here. Arrangements for Funerals . . .

FLINT: Right, carry on . . .

GINNY: Arrangements for the funeral, should be made as soon as possible . . .

FLINT: Go on then.

GINNY: That's all it says.

[FLINT *takes the book, peers at it, closes it, then tosses it on the sideboard*]

FLINT: Tck! Books. No wonder nobody reads em. I coulda writ that ruddy book meself!

GINNY: Shall I go and get Rene, then?

FLINT [*thinking deeply*]: Waittaminnit, waittaminnit, waait . . . Gin? We may be in dead lumber here . . . You said, YOU noticed, he was a bit dicky . . . Now think clearly Ginny my dear . . . How, dicky was he?

GINNY: Ever so dicky . . .

FLINT: *Real* dicky, you'd say . . .

GINNY: Yes, Jack.

FLINT: And yet, you didn't suggest that he saw the doctor?

GINNY [*trying to remember*]: Well . . . I did. I said, 'Look here Mister Merit, surgery don't finish till eight,' I said.

FLINT: What did he say?

GINNY [*remembering*]: Nothing. Well, when I said it like, he was getting a little bit of kipper off his back tooth with his little finger, and he just looked at it, then he went upstairs.

FLINT: Rrright! Now we're gettin' to the crucks of it. You offered him medical help, he picks his teeth, then slopes off up to his kip. You see, Gin, that *lea*gally constitoots a 'refusal'.

GINNY: Do it?

FLINT: Oh, YEH! Get me a pencil and paper!

[*She gets it*]

GINNY: Here y'are . . .

FLINT: I like all this legal work . . . [*Writing*] At 7-30, ayprocks . . . medical help was offered . . . sit down love . . . [*Leaning back*] You see Ginny . . . we are not wasting our time. You see, there is a law of the land, to cover everyfink, even dead lodgers.

GINNY: Is there?

FLINT: If we had a solicitor here, he'd probly uh . . . well . . . there'd probly be a 'Decease of the Lodgers Act' or sunnink . . . It'd be like the Factories Act you see, and it'd all be *there*, you know, in paras and subsections and so on . . . there'd be *his* rights and our rights, you see . . . Now, point one on the agenda, are we legally next of kin to him?

GINNY: I spose so . . .

FLINT: No. We stand in as land*lord*, and, uh, land*lady* . . . am I right or ain't I?

GINNY: Without a doubt!

FLINT: Good.

GINNY: What do we do now?

FLINT: Nuthink. [*Pacing*] Y'see Ginny . . . As soon as I step outta that door, darlin', it will inevidently follow that the authorities will swoosh into here like a pack of wolf-hounds. There'll be police, doctors, am'blances, off to the mortuary, coronorary inquest, official findings, paragraph in the local paper . . .

GINNY: Here! What're they gunna say up the road?

FLINT: They'll most likely hint at murder, knowing that lousy lot . . .

GINNY [*interested again*]: *She* will, in the corner shop!

FLINT: Quite! You see, we gotta tidy up a few odds and sods before I leave this house. Firstly we'll have to say he didn't pay us any rent.

GINNY: Ooo he did! I can remember. He give me two pound fifteen both Fridays. I had me hands in water both times . . .

FLINT: It'd be better if we said he paid no rent. I'll witness to that.

GINNY: All right Jack. He never paid.

FLINT: But what is more important, is when you INSISTED tonight, that he go down to the surgery, I shall witness that he refused!

GINNY: Well he *did!*

FLINT: Yes, but I shall witness it, [*winking*] because I was here. [*Chuckling*] This is the same as the old days in the army. Bein' on a fizzer!

GINNY [*just comprehending*]: Aoooh! Yeh. Witnessesses!

FLINT [*formally*]: You said to him that he oughter go down to the surgery, and he said he wouldn't bother, so I pleaded with him to see reason and he told me to mind me own business! [*Rising in anger*] Which is ruddy fohtuitous ennit? Here's us worrying our guts out about him, but to him, it's sans ferry annes, because all he's got to do is creep up to the comfort of his kip and snuff it, leaving US wiv all the bother! Now would *you* say that was a civilised action or not?

GINNY: No Jack!

FLINT: Dirty unconsiderate *bleee*der! It's enough to make yer loose your faif in yuman dignity Gin! That man has PUT on us! We offered him the hand of *friend*ship!

GINNY: He was sinister.

FLINT: Lousy upper-class git! You see Gin? He talked posh, wore a collar and tie *all* the week, made me, ME, feel inferior in me own gaff! I mean, reading the *Daily Telegraph*, and listening to all that diabolical music on the Third Programme? You woulda thought that made him a gentleman, but NO! When we come down to the pinch, he takes the ultimate heighth of liberties, which is to peg out on us! [*Deeply*] Oh Gin . . . it's very clear now. That man had no legal right whatsoever to decease on our rented premises. [*Going to kitchen*] It's a dead liberty . . . [*Indicating draining board*] I shall claim on his relatives for all this . . . I shall wanna bran'-new draining board ... [*Tearing down shelf*] And a new shelf ... [*Pacing back*] In fact, I shall probly want the whole place done out . . . [*He goes to the armchair and sits*]

GINNY [*looking round*]: It'd look nice in pink.

FLINT: So when we git to the coronorary inquest, we know what to say, okay?

GINNY: What will I say?

FLINT: You'll just belt up and agree with me.

GINNY: I will Jack.

FLINT: That's the best way, me old fruit. Teamwork. Stick together. Unity.

GINNY: Yes Jack.

FLINT: Because if you open your great 'ole in the wrong place we'll both be behind bars. Understood?

GINNY: Yes Jack.

FLINT: The remaining problem . . . [*Getting up and taking a shovel*]

GINNY [*leaping up*]: Eee Jack!

FLINT [*going to kitchen*]: Is to dispose of the body . . .

[*She screams. He studies her briefly, then gets some coke from a box under the gas stove, and comes back and shoves it on the fire*]

FLINT: Didn't you say he had a brother?

GINNY: He writ to him, the day before yesterday. He told me.

FLINT: It's the brother's job to get him buried. I tell you what, I ain't seein' any of our money go down a hole with brass handles on it!

GINNY: We ain't got any money.

FLINT: That's beside the point.

GINNY: Would—we be expected to go to his funeral?

FLINT: Not really, but still, it might make a nice day out for you, a nice break.

GINNY: Teddy's funeral, now that's the one I wished I coulda gone to.

FLINT: Well, you saw the photograph . . .

GINNY: Yeh, but I coulttn't tell which little cross was his.

FLINT: Well, all *right* then!

GINNY: How many would have gone to young Teddy's funeral?

FLINT: The padre and a few mukkahs I spose . . .

GINNY: Not many then?

FLINT [*truly sad, briefly*]: Not many mate . . . not many . . .

GINNY: Now if that was Teddy upstairs, instead of a stranger . . . it'd be different . . .

FLINT: Oh fer Gawd's sake, DO LEAVE OFF Gin! That's about the morbidest conversation you could ever have.

GINNY: I like to remember him!

FLINT: Yeh, well let's git off the subject.

GINNY: No, what I meant was, what a pity it is. You know, we never saw Teddy—after. And yet he was our own boy . . . [*Mouth trembling*] And, and—I mean we don't hardly know Mister Merit . . . [*She looks as though she is crying*]

[FLINT *studies her heartlessly*]

FLINT: I can see, that I shall have to follow the course, that Pontious the pilot did. I shall wash my hands of this affair. It's gettin' sentimental. [*Getting coat*] I shall nip round to Harry's and tap on the back door . . . I need a glass of stimmerlant!

GINNY: And I'll run down the road and tell the ginger sergeant that you're drinkin' after time!

FLINT [*darkly*]: Oh . . . it seems that I am not master in my own gaff tonight . . .

GINNY: Don't leave me here Jack, please!

FLINT: Then do what I tell you then . . .

GINNY: All right Jack.

FLINT: That's twice, I have politely requested you to shut your 'ole . . .

GINNY: I'm sorry love.

FLINT [*contentedly*]: Well then.

[*He paces back to his chair. He sits with some dignity. His legs fly up as he falls backward. The back rest stay is broken. He sits up with some dignity remaining*]

FLINT: I've broke me back!

GINNY [*flapping*]: Well the stick went and I tied it with wool!

FLINT [*with returning confidence*]: Ginny . . . you cannot mend a chair with wool . . . YOU NEED WIRE!

GINNY: Where can I get wire from!?

FLINT: I shall purloin some tomorrer. In fact, I'll nick a dirty great roll, they won't miss it, then you can fix everything. Here, and ANOTHER thing! Did he give us notice?

GINNY: Well he couldn't!

FLINT: Don't matter about that. We're entitled to notice, mate. His brother'll have to pay an extra week's rent. Right, that's all settled then Gin, and if you'll get the blanket, I can take me trousis off and warm me legs, and nip up to bed before the chill gets at me!

[*She goes automatically to get the blanket while he starts to take his trousers off*]

GINNY: We can't leave him in the house all night . . .

FLINT: Course we can!

GINNY: But doctors can tell. Like on telly, they take their

wrist and hold it and they say, 'he died, uhm,' they say, 'about eight hours ago'—or, if it was two hours, you know, they *know*, don't they?

FLINT: So what?

GINNY: Well, we'll git told off!

FLINT: What you on abaht *now*?

GINNY: Well, we ain't informed the—informed the inthorrit ... we ain't TOLD 'EM have we?

FLINT: I'll concede that ... [*He goes over quietly and thoughtfully and puts on his coat and does it up*] Siddown a minute ...

GINNY [*sitting*]: Where're you going?

FLINT: I want you to try to imagine, that I've just come home from work ...

[*He goes out of the hall door and comes in, she jumps up, does a lap round the table and hangs up his coat*]

FLINT: Now, I would sit down, and you would hand me the paper ...

GINNY [*doing this*]: What's all this for Jack?

FLINT: Jus' concentrate. Now I would speak ... [*Formally*] I have had a terrible bad day today. He has had us, humping them dirty greasy boxes, out of them filthy mucky mews again ... 'Oh dear' you'd remark ...

GINNY [*raptly*]: Oh dear!

FLINT: Then I'd say ... [*Formally*] 'How's *Fred*?'

GINNY: '*He* is gorn upstairs ...'

FLINT: 'Ho, *really*,' I'd reply. 'It's a bit *early* though, isn't *it*?'

GINNY: 'Well . . . he has come over a *trifle* dicky . . .'

FLINT: 'Hoh, *how* sad . . .'

GINNY: 'He *is* dead!'

FLINT [*leaping up*]: Oh give *over* Gin!

GINNY: Well, well, I——what're we tryin-a do Jack?

FLINT: I'm tryin' ter prove sunnink in a logical manner! I was trying to prove, that, we could be down here, and he could be up there, and we do not KNOW about him! [*Half crossing*] Is that crystal *clear* Virginia?

GINNY [*comprehending now*]: Aouh . . .

FLINT [*taking up paper*]: As far as we know, he is asleep. [*Starts to glance at it*]

GINNY: Yeh! I mean doctors are educated, and all that, but they coulttn't argue with that could they?

FLINT: What we ain't observed we can't report, can we?

GINNY: No.

[*He reads the paper. She sits hunched*]

GINNY [*tittering*]: Hee hee!

FLINT: You see?

GINNY: Yes! They'll have to hoo, hoo.

FLINT [*joining in laughter*]: Y'see, the daft sod'll have to hee hoo ha hurgh hurgh . . .

GINNY [*shrieking with laughter*]: OOH AH! They'll have to hee hee hoo hoo ha ha . . .

[*They have a good laugh and then feeling better, settle back with the odd chuckle, then silence*]

FLINT [*rustling paper*]: He can die in the morning, first thing . . . [*Rising*] I shall take him a cup of tea, [*mirthfully*] being a special occasion, and as soon as I have noted that he is fully clothed and not breaving, I shall call 'OY'.

GINNY [*rising, getting into the act*]: What, ever, is UP Jack?

[*They act the situation as before*]

FLINT: 'Mister Merit, does SEEM to have passed away in the night . . .'

GINNY: 'Hoh, my Gawd . . .'

FLINT [*going through door*]: 'He is most deffny morrybund. I should hasten to inform the old M.O. ducks . . .'

GINNY: 'I will, straightaway.'

FLINT: 'Cheery-BY then!'

GINNY [*normally*]: Where you going then?

FLINT: Well, I'm off to work ain't I, I can't take a month off for that bloke can I?

GINNY: Yeh, but what if doctor asts me lotsa questions?

FLINT: Just go all closed up. Just act indifferent, you know, how you do when I come home all full of beer and passion? [*Sadly*] Blimey, you're handy enough at it.

GINNY [*sorting it out aloud*]: So, you'll go to work, and I'll nip down and get doctor and I won't say nothing like, except, you took him up a cuppa tea and, there he was like, so I thought, like, and I'm not having *him in the house tonight*

Jack he's not a nice sorta man! [*Sharply*] I was sweeping under his bed last week, and me brush dropped in his tatchy case, and I opened it to get it out, and, I see this HORRIBLE book!

FLINT: *Git* it!

GINNY: I'd be scared to!

FLINT [*rolling one sleeve*]: Are you going to disobey me *agen*?

GINNY [*scuttling to door, then stopping*]: What if he should sit up while I was rummaging in his tatchy?

FLINT [*tiredly*]: Offer him a cuppa tea. Look, git that book down here, before I go bezeek!

[*She goes. He blows out air in a long exhalation, showing fear and worry for the first time. He goes to the sideboard and takes a long pull at a bottle of tonic wine, emptying it. She comes in with the case dangling on the end of a walking stick, she puts it on the table. He gets a billiard cue from behind the sideboard and taking up a playing stance at the table, flicks open both locks*]

FLINT: There we are, no fingerprints. [*Opening case with cue*] Now, we can scrutinate this here, horrible book. [*As* GINNY *goes to grab it*] No NO! Use a clorth . . .

[*She picks up the book with a tea cloth*]

FLINT: Get the fish knives . . . no I'll fetch em . . .

[*He turns out half a drawer of junk in one great handful to find the knives. Then he comes back and turns the pages over on the book using them as tweezers*]

GINNY: It's a diary y'see . . . [*Holding the book out she backs round to get under the light*]

FLINT: Read it out then gel.

GINNY [*reading*]: 'It is cold. I am constipated.'

FLINT: Kaw luv us! Fancy putting all that filf down!

GINNY [*reading*]: 'This is the fourth day that I have been constipated.'

FLINT: He's got it recurrent.

GINNY [*reading*]: 'Mr Flint is very left wing in his views . . .'

FLINT [*reacting proudly*]: Go on?

GINNY: 'He goes to union meeting twice a week . . .'

FLINT: Yeh . . .

GINNY: '. . . and comes home roaring drunk and raves about starting a bloody revolution . . .'

FLINT [*pride collapsing into horror*]: Well, that's right bleed'n language to put in a diary for ladies to read ennit?

GINNY: Here! [*reading*] 'I don't think Mrs Flint washes much . . .'

FLINT: Dirty, critical bleeder!

GINNY [*reading*]: 'Sunday . . . As I sit here . . . writing this . . . I think to myself . . . how lonely I am. This is the first time . . . in my life . . . that I have been out of work . . . and had no friends round me . . .' [*Looking up*] Must be sad Jack . . .

FLINT [*lugubriously*]: Yeuh, 'tis.

GINNY [*reading*]: 'Jack Flint is a good hearted man.'

FLINT: It's *Jack* now . . .

GINNY [*reading*]: 'What is wrong with him is . . . that he has a good brain . . . but he has not been taught enough. He pretends to hate the middle class, but really he is scared of them. His life ·. . . is a' [*peering*] 'a tradeje—tragedy, of ignorance . . .'

FLINT [*sniffing*]: Dunno what that means . . . [*Considerately*] I uh, think I'll nip up and straighten his leg . . . [*He goes to the door*]

GINNY: Here Jack! [*Reads*] 'Each time Flint comes home drunk, he shakes the bedsprings half the night . . . I could not sleep a—'

FLINT: Hold it!

[*He crosses with the dignity of restrained outrage. Taking the book from her, on the dish cloth, he bears it to the fire and tips it in slowly*]

FLINT: That will be enough of *that*. I shall scrutinise this man's belongin's . . .

GINNY [*taking out bundle of photographs*]: That's his brother, look, he showed me that. [*Taking photo off and putting at back of stack*] Here, what's this lady tied to a chair?

FLINT: Gimme *that*! [*Shocked, he looks at the rest of the pictures and then puts them on the fire*]

FLINT: Depravities . . .

GINNY [*rummaging*]: Here, what's this in this box?

FLINT: That's a hyperdommick syringe . . . I read abaht them . . .

GINNY: What's all these bottles?

FLINT [*peering at label*]: In-sulin. Yeh, that's what I read about. All them stoodents take it at their 'orrible orgies!

GINNY [*throwing bottle down*]: There!

FLINT [*taking up a sock with another in it*]: We housed a monster here Gin . . . It's lucky really that you're a bit on the ugly side . . .

GINNY: Yeh.

FLINT [*unrolling sock*]: With me out most evenin's . . .

[*Money falls out of the sock. A train hammers through sounding its whistle shriekingly. They crouch over the pile of notes like people in a trance as* FLINT *spreads out the fivers and pounds slowly*]

GINNY: I ain't never sin so such money in all my life!

FLINT: Look at this! Enough to buy a motor car . . .

GINNY: Must be a hundred pounds . . . all in the one lot . . . blimey, if we had all that we could pay back Mum what we borrered when we got married . . .

FLINT: He was a gentleman . . .

[*They look up to the spot where they always point to when referring to him with new respect, reverence. There is a bump from up there and* GINNY *clings to* JACK FLINT *suddenly*]

GINNY: Jack!

FLINT: That's a thump from his room! [*Panting*] Sash, sash winder, probly . . .

GINNY: It was the floor! I mean, if he's dead, how can he bump the floor?

FLINT: How the hell do I know! Go up and have a look!

GINNY: Me?

FLINT: Hurry, hurry ! ! !

GINNY: You flipp'n well go.

[*He goes to the door decisively, pauses, comes back*]

FLINT: I've done a day's work mate! It's not my job to run up and down stairs mate!

GINNY: If he's alive he enarf going to be wild about burning his diary and that!

FLINT: I'm entitled to burn it. It's phonographic. There's a law about it.

[*There is more muffled banging and she clings to him frightenedly*]

FLINT [*sniffing*]: Next door, pokin' the fire!

GINNY: That means Rene's back in! From bingo! Shoulttn't we go and tell her Jack? [*Flapping*] Look Jack, please mate, you take his tatchy upstairs while I run round fer Rene. [*Stuffing things back in case*] I mean, if we just TOLD some-body else Jack, it'd be better, because, you know, the more that know, the better it is, and I mean, she'll be up to bed in a minute!

[*She hurries to the window over the sink and opens it and calls*]

GINNY: Reneeeeee?

[*A train shunts, far off and hoots dismally*]

FLINT: OY!

GINNY: Yes Jack?

FLINT: C'mere.

GINNY [*shuffling in*]: What?

FLINT: Are you tryin' to run this house?

GINNY: No Jack.

FLINT: Well sid*down* then!

GINNY [*squatting*]: I'm frightened Jack. My heart's thumpin'.

FLINT: Jest ignore it.

GINNY: If we told Rene, she could witness.

FLINT: Witness what?

GINNY: That we'd told her.

FLINT: Brilliant!

GINNY: It'd all be open and above board!

FLINT: Typical.

GINNY: . . . that's what I thought . . .

FLINT: Give over!

GINNY: Sorry Jack . . .

[*He sits at the table*]

FLINT: Listen. [*Ponderously*] Item number two on the agenda, is that Mr. Merit is a gentleman of dodgy habits, but is a man of considerable means . . . [*Sternly*] He has there . . . the wherewithal for a first class, society funeral . . .

GINNY [*rising*]: Yes Jack—

FLINT: And he shall *have* it!

GINNY [*sitting again*]: Of course.

[*Rises, pacing thoughtfully*]

FLINT: Because . . . although . . . as I have said before . . . he is an upper-class git . . . he has . . . his rights. BUT! We on the other hand . . . have ours . . .

GINNY: Of course!

FLINT: And we are ENTITLED . . . to a modicum of compensation! A few nicker! Now I shall have to take a day off work termorrer to fix everything up, and I shall claim a day's money off him. We are entitled to a week's rent in lieu of notice, remember he never give us notice, and you're entitled to a coupla bottles of tonic wine to nurse you over the shock. I shall note it all down. [*Scribbling in book*] Com-pen-say-shun. Nine pound, fifteen.

[*He takes two fivers from the money in the case*]

GINNY: How did you work that out?

FLINT: In me head.

GINNY [*understanding somehow*]: I see . . .

FLINT: I shall put that money on the shelf, so's we don't get it mixed with his money. Got a coupla half crowns?

GINNY: By the clock. What's it for Jack!

FLINT [*tossing the coins in the case*]: His change.

[*He paces away contentedly*]

GINNY: I fink it's wrong to take a dead man's money.

FLINT [*overbearingly*]: We are merely claimin' compensation here and now, before Admirrality and Probate get their bleedin' hooks into it. Do you fink they're going to sort aht that poor man's affairs for nuffink?

GINNY: Will they?

FLINT: Time they've done counting it, he'll owe it to them in legal fees! Gin! Why should the poor be the only ones what do everyfink for nuffink? Eh?

GINNY: I don't *know*!

FLINT: The doctor'll take his bit, and the coroner and all that . . . I mean. Blimey, there's been more money made outta hard luck, than *ever* there was outta pleasure gel! I work hard mate, luggin' boxes about for a livin'—and everyone thinks I'm a beast of burden—but I got enough brains to work that one out! They're as 'ard as iron all of 'em, and they give nothing! They fink that people like us are a joke! [*Sitting contentedly*] Well, we got the laugh on *them* this time . . .

GINNY: We ain't ignorant.

FLINT: We bloody ain't, mate.

GINNY: I'm glad Rene never come in.

FLINT [*contentedly*]: See? So it's all worked out well. We'll discover poor old Fred in the mornin' and I'll spend a full day sortin' it all out for the poor fellah. Any-a that tea left?

GINNY [*rising*]: Might be . . .

[*There is an urgent banging at the door. She gets the case. FLINT slumps to his knees under the table. She dithers then shoves the case at the back of his armchair, pulling a blanket over it hurriedly. She kneels beside him. Silence*]

GINNY: What we kneeling for?

FLINT: Instink!

[*The knocks repeat*]

GINNY: That's a copper's knock!

FLINT: Nip that case upstairs!

GINNY: They always look through the letter box in *Z Cars*!

FLINT: Nosey sods . . .

[*They listen*]

GINNY: They'd see me go by . . .

FLINT: Bound to.

GINNY: If we got out the kitchen winder, and climbed up the drainpipe, we could go to bed . . .

FLINT: That's laughable!

GINNY: I fink they've gone away . . .

FLINT: Have a peep . . .

[*She gets up and tiptoes round the table and opens the door into the hallway a crack. She peeps. She grins*]

GINNY: Nobody there. If we go to bed Jack, we can say we was in bed. That's how we never heard the knock.

FLINT: Yeh! I mean, I can't be kippin' and listening out for knocks, can I?

GINNY: Come on then . . .

FLINT: I take the case, and we can bung it under his bed again . . .

[*He takes it and crosses to the hall door. She turns the light off. He goes out. There is a bang at the door again, and they both come back in the dark, slamming the door behind them. He strikes a match*]

FLINT: Ooooh my gawd, what did yer want to go and slam that door for?

GINNY [*putting light on*]: I got scared. It's a bloke in a bowler. I saw his reflection through the glass.

FLINT: C.I.D.! Answer it!

GINNY: I daren't!

FLINT: Quick!

[*He dashes to the fireplace, sticks the case on an upright chair, sits precariously in front of it, opens the evening paper and sits almost wrapped in it*]

GINNY [*off*]: Evening . . .

[*She shows in a young, nervy man, who takes off his bowler politely and regards* FLINT *who rustles his paper absorbedly*]

BROTHER: This is number nine?

FLINT: Always was. Who do you want?

BROTHER: Fred Merit.

FLINT: Well, my name's Flint, Guv . . .

BROTHER: They just said, you know . . . next door, they said he lodged here . . .

GINNY: *Mr* Merit! ?

BROTHER: Yes.

FLINT: He does lodge here.

BROTHER: Nice.

GINNY: Lodged here a fortnight now. Ever such a nice—

BROTHER: He wrote to me, well, you know, he gets depressed at times, and I come straight down on the train . . . I mean, I know how he gets . . .

FLINT: We noticed he was melancholic . . .

BROTHER: Ooh he does. Is he in?

FLINT: Is he in Gin, dear?

GINNY [*confusedly*]: Is he IN?

FLINT: He should be in because he's never out.

GINNY: Yes! [*Going to door*] He's always in, so I'll see if he *is* . . . [*She calls up the stairs*] Are you *in*, Mr Merit? [*She listens, artificially*].

FLINT [*rustling paper*]: Says here, that the wireless is going over to ninety per-cent music.

BROTHER: You wouldn't think there'd BE that much music . . .

GINNY: He ain't in.

FLINT: He must be out then.

BROTHER: Or asleep.

FLINT [*heartily*]: Yes! He likes his kip old Fred!

BROTHER: Always did. I'm his brother by the way.

GINNY [*extending her hand*]: Pleased to meet you . . .

FLINT: Why don't you call back in the morning mate? It's uh . . . [*glancing at clock*] gettin' on a bit . . .

GINNY: No! Go up and wake him! It's a pity to come all this way! [*Shoving him out to the hall*] It's just at the top of the stairs . . .

[*He goes*]

FLINT: That was dead brilliant!

GINNY: I wanna hide that tatchy! You look daft sittin' there!

[*She grabs the case and jiggles and shoves it into the side-board with much grunting*]

FLINT: Yeuh, [*grudgingly*] quite a good idea . . .

[*He stands whistling mournfully while she starts clearing the table*]

GINNY: Not bin a bad day out.

FLINT: It's bin quite salubrious . . .

[FLINT *goes to the door and listens*]

GINNY: I wonder if he'll notice that the tatchy is missin'?

FLINT [*sharply*]: Keep actin' natural! [*Crossing to her*] And fer Gawd's sakes Gin, don't forget, that we know nuthink about him!

[*The* BROTHER *comes in*]

BROTHER: He seems to have mislaid his case.

GINNY [*quickly-sharply*]: What case!

[FLINT *looks at her, and warns her with his eyebrows*]

FLINT: *How,* precisely, do you mean mate, mislaid it . . .

BROTHER: Well he must have done you see. I mean he has a syringe, and—

GINNY [*covering a gasp*]: I'll get the kettle on I think . . .

[*She goes, out of sight of the* BROTHER *and her face shows her fear mounting slowly*]

FLINT: Go on?

BROTHER: He's got this diabetes. He has to give himself . . . and, you know if he misses one he goes in a sort of coma.

FLINT [*blankly*]: Coma . . .

BROTHER: He's in one now.

FLINT: Oauw, that is nasty . . . It's sorta dangerous ennit?

BROTHER: Well, he ought to have the injection quickly. [*Panicking a bit now*] What I meant was, he might have left it in the toilet or something . . . only I didn't want to go rummaging around *your* place, like.

FLINT [*gravely*]: I'll uh, I'll sort of have a bit of a shufti . . . [*Calls*] All right Gin?

GINNY: Yes, Jack!

[FLINT *goes out slowly.* GINNY *brings in her cup and saucer and tries to keep her face away from the* BROTHER, *then turns to him with a brave effort*]

GINNY: This is our living room, it's a bit—

BROTHER: Unusual shape!

GINNY: It's bin built in the skew.

BROTHER: Yes, on the angle . . .

GINNY: It makes it unusual.

BROTHER: That's, uh—that's one thing I love, you know, anything that's unusual . . .

GINNY [*turning away*]: Good.

[*She ducks down and gets the picture of her son from under the sideboard*]

GINNY: That was our Teddy, only the string went.

BROTHER: He looks fit!

GINNY: They trained his muscles, all up!

BROTHER: He looks sunburnt!

GINNY: Yes, well it was took at Skegness!

BROTHER: Where is he now?

GINNY: Oh, he's dead now.

BROTHER: Oh, I'm . . . I thought he . . . you know the way you . . .

[FLINT *comes in solemnly*]

FLINT: Yerse, he does deffny seem to be in a case of coma . . . [*Sniffing*] Funny thing . . . I don't seem to reckerleck, recalling any tatchy case.

BROTHER: What did he have when he came?

GINNY: Paper *bag*!

BROTHER: Where is it then?

FLINT: How should we know?

F

GINNY: We don't know what he had, we don't know nuffink about him!

BROTHER: He MUST have had SOMETHING!

FLINT: Oy, you'd just better watch your bleet'n alleygations mate!

GINNY: So you can stop making up accywe-accusay-*lies* about us *mate*!

BROTHER: For God's sakes! Look! I'm not accusing anyone of anything!

GINNY: Well you'd better not start.

FLINT: 'Cos I've got an evil temper!

BROTHER: HE NEEDS A DOCTOR! [*Shocked silence*] That's all . . .

GINNY: Oh, I see.

BROTHER: I know all this is a shock to you. I'm not blaming anybody . . . It's just that he has to have this injection quickly . . .

FLINT [*understanding*]: Aouw . . . 'scuse me pal. I uh, just sorta went terra firma with the shock of it . . .

GINNY: So did I.

FLINT [*leading* BROTHER *out*]: The old M.O. is just down the road there, five doors down . . .

[*The* BROTHER *goes. They stand still for a second or two staring past each other. Then they both move sharply.* FLINT *grabs the shovel while she gets the case. He hurries out to the kitchen and puts some coke to one side and she drops the case*

*among the coke. He shovels the coke on top. They hurry back
to the main living part. She sits on the pouffe and he beckons
for her to get up. He moves her to an upright chair by the
table*]

Sit here!

[*He grabs the paper and settles down in his chair and opens
it and pretends to be reading it*]

GINNY: He's fatter in the face, than Fred . . .

FLINT: Don't forget our story!

GINNY: No dear.

[*They wait patiently for a few seconds then they hear
voices outside.* FLINT *bends to his paper while the* BROTHER
brings the DOCTOR *in*]

BROTHER: Here's the Doctor, can we go up?

FLINT: You know the way, mate!

[*They go up.* FLINT *and* GINNY *sit absolutely still, briefly,
then* FLINT *goes to listen at the hall door*]

GINNY [*following him*]: Here, we shoulda hid that case upstairs,
while he was gone down the road . . .

FLINT: Where?

GINNY: In the karzi.

FLINT: Too small. Anyway, you said he had a paper bag! You
gotta stick to one story Ginny, otherwise they'll have yer!

GINNY: Shall we say about, him being dicky over tea?

FLINT: Yus!

GINNY [*sincerely*]: I was really worried about him Jack.

FLINT: Of course you were, Virginia my darlin' . . .

GINNY: So don't forget to witness what I say!

FLINT: Teamwork Gin . . . PULL TOGEVVUH! Okay?

[*Hearing footsteps they hurry softly back to their seats. The* DOCTOR *comes in*]

DOCTOR: His brother wants to stop upstairs briefly. Well, it's puzzling about this syringe . . . he must have had it somewhere!

FLINT [*rising*]: Evenin' Doctor!

GINNY [*rising*]: We was ever so worried about him tea time.

DOCTOR: Why was that?

GINNY: Well, he come over all sort of moribund . . .

DOCTOR: What do you mean exactly?

FLINT: He looked proply dicky, Doctor! I recall, remarking on it—to him—Doctor! I said, 'you need a doctor' Doctor.

DOCTOR: Why didn't you call me?

GINNY: He dittn't want to know. Look I even offered him these two tablets.

FLINT: I can witness that!

GINNY: You weren't here *then*, were you?

FLINT: Gin, I was in. Then I wen' out. Then I come in again. You can check that with the union, Doctor!

DOCTOR: There's no need to.

GINNY: That's right! I can witness that! He wen' out, and so I sat here worryin'.

DOCTOR: There's no need to be doing all this witnessing. Just tell me exactly what happened.

FLINT: He refused treatment! I can remember his words.

DOCTOR: What was said?

FLINT: I can't remember what was said. I just recall he was cattygorickal!

GINNY: Jack said, you want to go down to the surgery, and he said he dittn't like doctors!

FLINT: That's perfickly correct!

GINNY: He looked real groggy y'see!

FLINT: Terrible, he looked!

GINNY: Then he sorta, dragged hisself upstairs . . .

DOCTOR: Carry on.

FLINT: And I went out to the union, because I'm the *Hon* seckertarry . . .

DOCTOR: And you?

GINNY: I put the telly on.

DOCTOR: And it didn't occur to either of you to call me?

FLINT: Well, that ain't our—

DOCTOR: And yet I'm only five doors away!

GINNY: Yehm, but you'd be having a sit down . . .

FLINT: I said to *her*, Doctor . . . I said 'The doctor's had a hard day, he probly just having a sit down now . . .'

GINNY: Putting your feet up!

DOCTOR: And yet you thought he was dangerously ill!

FLINT: Terrible! [*Realising craftily*] Quite rough. What I mean is, he looked rougher than he was, if you get my meaning. Well you know Doctor . . . the army . . . [*Winking*] Malingering . . .

DOCTOR: Well, he's dead now. And he hasn't been dead very long. If only you people had just thought to come down . . . Half an hour ago, I could have saved him! Don't you realise that?

GINNY: We do now . . .

DOCTOR: Well, I must call an ambulance. You'll have to wait for the police, I'm afraid . . .

GINNY: We haven't done anything!

DOCTOR: Not directly, you haven't . . .

FLINT: I don't reckon it's *our* responsibility . . .

DOCTOR: Well then, you've got nothing to worry about . . .

[*He goes closing the hallway door behind him*]

FLINT: Good! We're in the clear. We gotta get rid of that case, now the nick's comin'! Poke the fire up!

[*She does this while he drags the case out. They kneel opening it*]

GINNY: Put the papers on first, to make a blaze. What will we do with the money?

FLINT: Oo Gawd . . .

GINNY: We can't take it!

FLINT: We got to, Gin!

[*He stands holding the money while she pokes letters on the fire. Behind his back, the hall door opens slowly*]

GINNY: I feel terrible. We've murdered that bloke . . .

FLINT: Tell you what. We won't keep the money . . .

[*The* BROTHER *comes in, his eyes wet, hardly able to believe what he sees*]

BROTHER: That's his case.

GINNY: It's an old box!

FLINT: It's some rubbish we're gettin shot of!

BROTHER: You liars!

FLINT: Watchit mate! We're both witnessin' each uvver!

BROTHER: You just said you murdered him!

[GINNY *leaps forward from her kneeling position grabbing the* BROTHER's *legs and as he falls she crouches over him with the syringe held aloft the needle glittering over his eyes*]

GINNY: Say that again!

FLINT: Gin-NY!

[*He pulls her away, holding her arm. She looks ready to do murder now*]

GINNY: He's a filfy rotten liar! We ain't done nothing bad!

FLINT: Simmer dahn Gin. [*To* BROTHER] You? Out!

BROTHER [*going*]: I shall find a policeman!

FLINT: You do that, mate!

[GINNY *goes back to the fireplace, while* FLINT *tosses the wad of money all over the table*]

The place'll be teemin' with bogies now! We'll be up half the night!

GINNY: I bet they twist every single word what we tell 'em.

FLINT: Course they will. That's the way the officer class works!

GINNY: Can we say, I mean, why was we burning his little tatchy?

FLINT: Because we'd run outta coke, how should I know!

GINNY: Say we found it, and we thought, you know—we never knew it was his and we was burning it . . . it was all filfy, and we thought we might ketch something off of it?

FLINT: A judge and jury would tiddle 'emselves, laughing at that one! [*Tiredly*] Yuck, I dunno any more. My bonce is goin' round in circles. They're all ganged up.

GINNY: Who?

FLINT: Them! They all earn the big money. They wouldn't wanna know. Don't think that lawyers and conorarry inquests and all that have to sit up to tea wiv lodgers every night do you? Just for a bit of beer money.

GINNY: We won't have no more lodgers. Here! Then we can have supper on our own. I could get two little trays . . . we wouldn't have to sit up the table any more . . . We could eat it off our laps . . . and Jack, if you stopped in some nights, there's some SMASHIN' programmes on! There's love stories and—

FLINT: Love? What you on about then? The other?

GINNY: No . . . I never meant real love . . . I meant . . . nice love . . . you know . . .

[*He puts his arm round her, kisses her roughly, then walks away embarrassedly*]

FLINT: You're a real right comic!

[*He shakes his head*]

GINNY: W–ell?

FLINT: What do we want to be doin' with love stories? That's all upper–class stuff . . .

GINNY: Tell you what has bin nice . . . Us talking all this much. We ain't talked so much since we was told that Teddy died . . .

FLINT: It's a dyin' art—the old conversation. [*Prodding telly*] That fing's killed it! I'm not stupid mate. That's why I go dahn the boozer and keep up the art of arguin'!

GINNY: What about, arguin'?

FLINT: About them and us mate! [*Putting his arm round her shoulder*] Y'see mate, there's them and us, and they got their way, and we got our way, and—

GINNY: They're different? Posher . . .

FLINT [*correcting her*]: Harder. Y'see . . . it ain't no good telling them anythink else than a pack of lies Gin, because they wouldn't expect it mate . . . by Gawd, I'd have liked to have bin an educated lawyer . . .

GINNY: You'd have bin one of the best!

FLINT: I'd a bin . . . a sort of Robin Hood in a barrister's outfit . . .

GINNY: It woulda suited you, with your big shoulders . . .

FLINT: It ruddy would mate!

GINNY: You woulda bin the best.

FLINT: Yeh . . .

GINNY: And you woulda bin mine . . .

FLINT: Yeh . . .

GINNY: Yeh . . .

FLINT: Yeh . . .

GINNY: Yeh!

FLINT: YEH!

GINNY: YEH!

[*The curtain falls slowly during the last six exchanges*]

THE END

The Gift

RONALD DUNCAN

CAST

<small>PERCY WORSTHORNE</small>—a bank clerk aged 59
<small>MADELAINE WORSTHORNE</small>—his wife aged 50
<small>ERNEST TREMLETT</small>—her father aged 73
<small>TONY WORSTHORNE</small>—their son aged 25
<small>GERALDINE WORSTHORNE</small>—their daughter aged 23
Voice of <small>TV</small>
Voice of <small>RADIO</small>

The Gift

SCENE: *What is known as a living room. But there is no window:
just a door, a few uncomfortable chairs, a* RADIO *and a* TV *set
which are set one each side of the proscenium in the style of a
Greek chorus. No walls are necessary for the set: a hung
picture or two will define the room's limits. The only
essential prop is an enormous parcel. It measures 6' long by 3'
high by 2' wide. This is wrapped in brown paper. A small
birthday cake with one candle is also conspicuous on a side
table.*

Throughout the action, the TV *and* RADIO *pursue their
irrelevant and frivolous commentaries—or, at least, they do so
at times as counterpoint.*

When the curtain rises, MRS WORSTHORNE *is tying a
large blue ribbon round the parcel; the others watch her from
the other side of the room.*

Time: the present.

TV SET: Leeds United	3	Chelsea	2
Manchester City	1	Bolton Wanderers	0
Bradford City	3	Liverpool	2
Charlton Athletic	4	Hull City	3
Fulham	2	Tottenham Hotspur	2
Arsenal	1	Southampton	1
Blackpool	1	York City	6
Aston Villa	5	Coventry	2

. . . [*ad lib.*]

MADELAINE: Doesn't it look pretty?
I think it looks very pretty.
Percy will like this, blue's his favourite colour.
Did you know blue was his favourite colour?
Well, there it is. Doesn't it look magnificent?
Doesn't it?

TONY: Yes.

GERALDINE: It does.

MADELAINE: Don't you think so, Daddy?

[*The two women begin to set the tea*]

TV SET: Woolwich   2   Middlesboro'   2

TREMLETT [*marking football pools*]: What?

TONY: Mother said: doesn't it look magnificent?

TREMLETT: That's another draw: And on their home ground.
Yes. It does. It looks magnificent but . . .

MADELAINE: But . . . ?

TREMLETT: But I think it is too big.
I suppose there will be another week, next week.

MADELAINE: As it couldn't be any smaller
It is not very helpful of you
To remark that it is too big.

RADIO: To-day for our programme *Any Questions*
the team consists of . . . [*ad lib.*]

TV SET: Worthington makes you worthier and worthier
. . . [*ad lib.*]

GERALDINE [*to her mother*]: You've got a point there.

TREMLETT: No, only six this week. Twelve draws.

TONY: Yes, Mother is right. It isn't meaningful
To discuss the size of a thing
Without relating the size to the function.
Some people might say that the Pacific Ocean was big,
But it is not big when you consider
The amount of water it has to contain.

TREMLETT: I still say it is big, too big.

TONY: Yet it may prove too small.

GERALDINE: That would be a pity.

TONY: After the expense we've all been put to.

MADELAINE [*to* TONY]: Don't worry. Your mother may not
be a Bachelor of Science
As we all know you are.
[To GERALDINE] Nor is she about to take her Diploma
In Psychiatric Nursing. But your mother is practical.
She took precautions: I used a tape measure.

GERALDINE: Must we go into details?

TREMLETT: Too big for this room, I mean.

MADELAINE: I am sure Percy will be pleased with it.
Eventually. I am sure no man has ever received
A more appropriate birthday present.
Or one to which his family has given so much thought.
Now what shall we put on the card?

GERALDINE [*impulsively*]: Many happy returns ... [*They look
shocked*] Sorry.

TONY: 'For Percy. With our undying love.' Then all of us
sign it.

MADELAINE: Splendid. That's it. [*She writes*] 'Undying love'.
I'll underline that.
He'll like that.
There now, sign it.

[*They all do so then she ties the card on to the parcel*]

Percy will never guess what it is.
Last year I gave him an electric razor
Or was that the year before last? I forget.
Now, Tony, help me to put this screen round it.
Your father enjoys a surprise.

[*They do so*]

TREMLETT: The year you'll remember.

MADELAINE: We'll all remember. We all subscribed to it.
As a family what else could we do:
Once we had realised what he really wanted or needed?

TREMLETT: I could have given him an ounce of tobacco.

MADELAINE: You could have given him an ounce of tobacco,
And I could have given him a handknitted tie.
They could have given him a book token
Or a long playing gramophone record.
But those would have been frivolous gestures of affection
And what we have given him here is something more than a
    casual gift.
It is a real token of love, our undying love.

GERALDINE: Something he needed, but couldn't give himself.

TONY: Something he needed, but didn't know he wanted.
What else could we do?

MADELAINE: Nothing.

GERALDINE: Nothing. He's certainly **not** certifiable.
You have my word for that.

TONY: But assuredly as mad as a hatter.

MADELAINE: Tony, don't speak of your father like **that**.
Though I admit his behaviour is far from sane
Ever since he resigned from his job at the bank
[*bitterly*] Only four months before his pension!

TONY: I still can't believe it.

TREMLETT: After thirty years: four months before his pension!

MADELAINE: To be precise; three months and seventeen days.

[*Pause*]

Ever since that day, when he marched in here one after-
noon,
With his valise full of poems which he blandly admitted
That he had written in the bank's time and on the tills
And announced that he had resigned his job
Because he had suddenly realised that he'd misspent his life
Counting bits of paper there,
And that he was now going to devote the rest of his days
To important things such as persuading people to read
poetry
(which they will never do)
And urging them to love one another
(which they can never do).
As I say ever since that dreadful day, we have all known
That he would soon need more than a handknitted tie
Or an ounce of tobacco.

TREMLETT: Two ounces. I always gave him two for his
birthday.

GERALDINE: Yes. What else could we do? I didn't mind
His sudden enthusiasm for poetry.
A lot of people write poetry,
Some people even read poetry.
And some people keep bees; others tropical fish in aerated
tanks;
There's no accounting for tastes.
But what I thought indicated that he's gone over the top
—And I'm not without professional experience—
Was when his manic depressive moods
Fluctuated between such irrational irreconcilable extrem-
ities.

TONY: Precisely.

GERALDINE: His moments of despair were reasonable enough;
Few of us can see any hope.
To me it's his moods of joyful optimism
Which prove he's now completely ga-ga.

MADELAINE: Geraldine! A spade's a spade
You don't have to call it a bloody shovel!
He is your father.

GERALDINE: That's why I'm so concerned for his future
And why I've contributed to that.
Do you know, Mother, I actually caught him at it yesterday.

MADELAINE: Where?

GERALDINE: In Chelsham Road. I had been to see Betty . . .

TONY: Does it matter whom you'd been to see?
Keep to the point. What was Father doing?

GERALDINE: Going from house to house like a self-employed
postman

Without any letters. He was singing gaily
And skipping over the railings which divide the front
    gardens.
You can guess what he was doing.
He was popping a copy of Keats' *Ode to a Nightingale* into
    every letter box.
I asked him what good he thought that would do!
And d'you know what he said?
He said: 'I'm blowing their indifference up.
Poetry is more powerful than an atom bomb.'

TONY: It's sad.

TREMLETT: Very.

GERALDINE: And clear that he is no longer in touch with
    reality.

MADELAINE: Very clear. Think of the cost of printing all
    those copies.

TREMLETT: What convinced me he was barmy was when he
    turned the greenhouse
Into a carpenter's shop
And started to make those boards he carries.
Better if they'd been used for a straitjacket.

[*Singing heard off*]

MADELAINE: Ssh. Here he comes.

[*Enter* PERCY *still singing gaily. He is wearing a sandwich
board which reads 'Love one another'*]

Have you had a good day, dear?

[PERCY *nods, takes the sandwich board off, and props it up.*

We now see the other side; it reads 'Read Donne. Listen to Schubert']

GERALDINE [*going to embrace him*]: Many happy . . .

TONY [*going to embrace him*]: I hope you have a happy day, Father.

PERCY: Thank you, my boy, I have.
I am having the happiest day of my life.
D'you know what I've done today?

MADELAINE [*fearfully*]: No, Percy. What have you done?

PERCY: I have stood all the afternoon in the High Street
Outside the bank, my bank.
And I sang (Schubert of course)
And I gave a five pound note to everybody who stopped to give me a penny.
It was a wonderful business. You should have seen their faces.
Two women kissed me from gratitude.

MADELAINE: Expensive kisses. How much did you give away?

PERCY: Two hundred pounds or so.
It made my colleagues in the bank look pretty foolish.

MADELAINE: So I can imagine, dear. Half our savings.

PERCY: Not quite. I've enough for tomorrow too.
People seemed most grateful. I daresay they'd overspent
On their summer holidays. Of course some thought my notes were counterfeit
They took them into the bank and were soon disabused
Because I'd drawn them out from there this morning.
And there were one or two who paused before they folded the note into their wallet.

These may in time realise that I was not merely giving
  away fivers
But values.

TONY: New lamps for old.

PERCY: Exactly. I'm hoping one or two others will join me
  at it tomorrow.
  We must cast our bread upon the water,
  And if we haven't any bread, then paper has to do.
  There's no alternative, otherwise it turns to stone; we turn
  to stone
  It's simple.

MADELAINE: Yes, dear.

PERCY [*looking at table*]: Well, where is it? I've been looking
  forward all day to my present.
  Let me guess what it is. Don't tell me.
  Some tobacco from Dad?

MADELAINE: Not this year, dear.
  This year we all clubbed together.
  To give you something special
  Something you needed.

PERCY: A screwdriver and a plane?

MADELAINE: No.

PERCY: A handknitted tie? Perhaps two?

GERALDINE: No.

PERCY: Clubbed together. That's a clue.
  A Schubert Song Cycle?

GERALDINE: It's not fair, Mummy. He'll never guess. Remove
  the screen.

[*They do so*]

MADELAINE: There.

TREMLETT: Big. I say it's too big.

[PERCY *walks round it then reads the card attached*]

PERCY: I was right you see:
Generosity is more contagious than measles.
But I can't think what it is.

GERALDINE: Try.

PERCY: Something I need? . . . A printing press?

TREMLETT: For fivers?

PERCY: Poetry.

MADELAINE: Cold.

PERCY: A loudspeaker outfit?

MADELAINE: Still cold.

[PERCY *walks round it again*]

PERCY: A coffin?

MADELAINE: No. But you're getting warm.

GERALDINE: Mother, Daddy will never guess.

[*She goes and undoes the ribbon then rips the paper*]
It's a deep freeze.

MADELAINE: The latest model. Made in Sweden.

PERCY [*peering into it*]: It's magnificent. Thank you.
But we have a refrigerator already.
We bought it only last year. It was all right this morning.

TONY: A deep freeze is not the same thing as a refrigerator.

PERCY: Similar surely?

TONY: A model like that will keep things indefinitely.
I knew a man who put a whole salmon in one.
After ten years, after ten years, it came out
As the day he'd poached it.

PERCY: A pity I don't fish or poach.

TONY: Indefinitely. Or you can put peas, beans and raspberries
in them.
At fifty degrees below zero decomposition is arrested.

PERCY: But I haven't a vegetable garden.

TONY: Pheasants. Some people put pheasants in them.

PERCY: So would I if I owned a shoot.

GERALDINE: You don't understand, Daddy.
Any meat will keep in them for ever.

PERCY: A marvellous thing if I were a butcher or a farmer.
As it is I hope you won't be offended
If I exchange it for a printing press, or something.
[*To* MADELAINE] I can't think what I could put in it, can
you dear?

MADELAINE: Yes, Percy. I can.

PERCY: What?

MADELAINE: Yourself, dear.

PERCY: Myself?

MADELAINE: You've talked so much recently about permanent values
And immortal life. This can give these to you.

TONY: It certainly can. Suspended animation.

GERALDINE: Indefinitely, Daddy.

PERCY: I see you are joking. [*He laughs alone*]
I see you are not joking.

MADELAINE: No, dear.
Of course we thought of several things we could have
given you.
At first Geraldine suggested a carpentry set with an electric
drill
And Tony proposed a press for your trousers
But we discarded these ideas as frivolous
Because we all realised that you were no longer interested
In things or in appearances . . .

TONY: . . . either sartorially or philosophically
But only in the reality behind things.
And so, Mother suggested we should give you something
you needed . . .

MADELAINE: Something you really wanted
And this can give you immortal life
In a way no religion can.
The manufacturers guarantee it.

PERCY: I must say I've never had such a big present before.
All the same I feel a little depressed by it.

GERALDINE: You shouldn't be, Daddy.
Think of the mammoths.

PERCY: Why? I don't hunt mammoths either.

GERALDINE: Because a few years ago they unearthed an
entire mammoth in Siberia.
I read about it in one of the Sunday papers.

Apparently the beast had been overtaken by the last Ice Age
And frozen to death while grazing on the steppes.
Its mouth was still full of grass. And d'you know
When it thawed out, it was still so fresh
That it bled when they cut steaks from it
Which they found succulent after ten thousand years?
Think of that, Daddy, ten thousand years
Of assured preservation.

PERCY: Which of you wants to eat me?

TREMLETT: It's big, but not that big.
You wouldn't get much of a mammoth in that one.

MADELAINE [*pacifying* TREMLETT]: It will be the time for the
News soon, Dad.
Just you sit quiet and wait.

PERCY: This must have cost you all a great deal.
I can't countenance such extravagance . . .

MADELAINE: You should talk.

PERCY: . . . For myself. I'm sure the shop will exchange it
For some modest necessity or indulgence.
I really do need a set square, and some screws.

TONY: Nonsense, Dad. Think of Cleopatra, or Helen of Troy.

PERCY: Why, Tony?

TONY: Think how you would have liked to have made love
To either or both of them.

MADELAINE: Tony!

PERCY: Since they are both dead and since I am both a realist
and a monogamist,
At least in practice, I have never considered such liaisons.

TONY: No, but what I'm trying to tell you is:
Suspended animation makes such unlikely unions possible,
At least theoretically. If Cleopatra had stepped into a model
  like that
Instead of sucking an asp, she could have skipped 2,000
  years
And woken to embrace you as another Antony
In your strong toil of grace.

PERCY: A somewhat unlikely hypothesis.

TONY: Maybe. But they've proved that the male seed
When frozen to 80° can remain potent indefinitely.

GERALDINE: I can't see where this is getting us.

TONY: Don't you? This deep freeze assures physical immort-
  ality
Completely.
Theoretically, Dad could, if he takes this step,
Father a child five centuries from now.
—By artificial insemination if need be.
Not of course from Cleopatra, but on some unborn film
  star.
You could say that a deep freeze like that
Is a sort of Savings Bank
For a man's generative potential . . .

MADELAINE: I don't think that description will appeal to
  your Father
But I believe I know what will persuade him.
Percy, you threw up your job
Because you became interested in real and permanent values
  in life,
Didn't you?

PERCY: Yes.

MADELAINE: Then surely it's reasonable for you to take steps
To preserve those values permanently.
You explained that your enthusiasm for poetry
Was because you saw it as the highest point of human
consciousness,
And you said that we should love one another
As being the only way to express that consciousness, didn't
you?
You were right. None of us could disagree with you there.
But Percy, you are before your time, a thousand years
Before your time, maybe even more.
Today nobody will listen to you, even if you give them
fivers.
The golden age of poetry is passed
And nowadays people don't love one another, but occasion-
ally
Hate each other intimately and passionately in corners.
In spite of what they say, they are only interested in
appearances
And in labels, not in realities.
So you see, if you value your values, Percy, you must
wait;
You must preserve yourself and them
Then wake to an Age that will listen to your message:
That poetry is the way to consciousness
As love is the way to joy.

GERALDINE: Mother, I've never known you so articulate
before;
The occasion has inspired you.
She is right, Daddy. Logically, there is no alternative for
you:

If you continue as you are, you will die, as we all die,
With your values tarnished and your hopes dead with you.
You will eventually become as hopeless as we are.
Can't you see we want you to do this, not for your good
But for ours?
It's true that today poets and priests look hopeless and
    ridiculous figures
But for all that they are our only points of hope.
We must preserve you somehow.

PERCY: Your logic closes in on me like a prison.

GERALDINE [*running to embrace him*]: Daddy, you know I love
    you; you know I shall miss you
And miss the poem you write especially for me
Every Christmas . . .
I couldn't bear the thought of you dying
And what you stand for dying, too.
That's why I want to preserve you
That's why I want you to step in there.

MADELAINE [*to* TONY]: If anybody can persuade him, she will.
    He'll do anything for her.

TONY [*bitterly*]: I know.

PERCY [*to* GERALDINE]: I've already started to write something
    for you for next Christmas
But it's not finished.

TONY: A poem never is finished
    A poem is a point of growth.

MADELAINE [*aside to* TONY]: Clever. [*To* PERCY] Well, Percy?
    [*She gets a pillow*]Shall we make you comfortable?

PERCY: It will be cold in there.

MADELAINE [*taking his hand*]: Colder for us outside when you
    can no longer warm us.

PERCY [*looking at her hand*]: That was your best argument.
    But I will not get in this thing to preserve myself
    Or anything which I stand for:
    Either the bad poem I am writing,
    Or the good poem I hope one day to write.

GERALDINE [*petulantly*]: Oh Daddy. How disappointing!

MADELAINE [*angrily*]: What a waste of money!

PERCY: Nor will I get into it to escape from the loneliness
    Of growing old, or from the humiliation
    Of being old. Or to evade the paralytic stroke,
    The fatal motor accident or the cancer we nurture
    That takes us unaware: though these fears are real fears.
    I will not get into it because I am dying—
    Because that it is what we are all doing—
    Dying as we wear a new handknitted tie.

TONY: Most disappointing. We shall drop 20% on it.

PERCY [*taking his coat off*]: But I will get into it because it was
    a gift from your love
    It is that love alone which is worth preserving.
    If I stand here, I reject that love
    [*he steps in*] But in here, I accept it.
    It's cold; but not so cold as I feared.
    Perhaps it was only my fear that was cold?

MADELAINE [*handing a scarf to him*]: Put this on, dear.

GERALDINE: Don't be silly, Mother.

MADELAINE: And he never had a slice of his cake. [*She goes to cut a piece*]

PERCY [*almost to himself*]: I can't feel my hands: I cannot feel my feet
My closest friends are lost:
It is in our extremities that we are vulnerable;
But what matters, if in our hearts we are secure?

[*They gather round*]

GERALDINE: Is the thermostat switched on?

TONY: Full.

TREMLETT: Not too big, I was wrong there.

GERALDINE: Oh Daddy, first recite something to me
Like you used to do when you came to sit on my bed
When I was a girl. Please, Daddy.
Oh, his lips are going blue.

PERCY [*sitting up*]: What, darling—one of the odes?
The *Ode to a Nightingale*?

GERALDINE: No. Something of your own—
The poem you were writing for me for Christmas.

PERCY: If love is made of words
          Who can love more than I?
          If love is all self-love
          Who's more beloved than I?

          If love is made of faith
          Who can love less than I?
          If love is to submit
          Who's less beloved than I?

If love is made of tears
    Who could love more than she?
If love is to betray
    Who . . .

[*His lips move completing the poem but no sound is emitted.*
They lie him down]

TV SET: Bolton Wanderers 2   Sheffield United 3
Leeds United 4   Liverpool 3

. . . [*ad lib. to end*]

[*The family now turn to face the audience as though looking*
through a window]

TONY: Strange: I see they are playing tennis next door
And sitting out in deck chairs: but I feel cold: very.

TREMLETT: Me too. There the roses lean upon the evening
But frost feathers my brain, icicles nail my heart.
Now I know what you meant by them mammoths.

MADELAINE: I see my Michaelmas Daisies need tying up
That proves it is summer still
Though winter is within us.

GERALDINE: His greenhouse door needs mending.
[*To herself*] 'If love is to betray
Who was more loved than He?'

TV SET: Blackpool 1   Exeter 2

[*etc.*]

THE END